DUNDE

Champions of Scot

1961-62

DESERT ISLAND FOOTBALL HISTORIES

CLUB HISTORIES	ISBN
Aberdeen: A Centenary History 1903-2003	1-874287-49-X
Aberdeen: Champions of Scotland 1954-55	1-874287-65-1
Aberdeen: The European Era – A Complete Record	1-874287-11-2
Bristol City: The Modern Era – A Complete Record	1-874287-28-7
Bristol City: The Early Years 1894-1915	1-874287-74-0
Cambridge United: The League Era – A Complete Record	1-874287-32-5
Cambridge United: 101 Golden Greats	1-874287-58-9
The Story of the Celtic 1888-1938	1-874287-15-5
Chelsea: Champions of England 1954-55	1-874287-77-5
Colchester United: Graham to Whitton – A Complete Record	1-874287-27-9
Coventry City: The Elite Era – A Complete Record	1-874287-51-1
Coventry City: An Illustrated History	1-874287-59-7
Dick Duckworth: Manchester United's Edwardian Hero	1-874287-80-5
Dundee: Champions of Scotland 1961-62	1-874287-86-4
Dundee United: Champions of Scotland 1982-83	1-874287-71-6
History of the Everton Football Club 1878-1928	1-874287-14-7
Halifax Town: From Ball to Lillis – A Complete Record	1-874287-26-0
Hereford United: The League Era – A Complete Record	1-874287-18-X
Hereford United: The Wilderness Years 1997-2004	1-874287-83-X
Huddersfield Town: Champions of England 1923-1926	1-874287-66-X
Ipswich Town: The Modern Era – A Complete Record	1-874287-43-0
Ipswich Town: Champions of England 1961-62	1-874287-63-5
Kilmarnock: Champions of Scotland 1964-65	1-874287-87-2
Luton Town: The Modern Era – A Complete Record	1-874287-05-8
Luton Town: An Illustrated History	1-874287-37-6
Hatters Centurians: 100 Appearances for Luton Town	1-874287-79-1
Matt Busby: A Complete Manchester United record 1946-1969	1-874287-53-8
Motherwell: Champions of Scotland 1931-32	1-874287-73-2
Norwich City: The Modern Era – A Complete Record	1-874287-67-8
Peterborough United: The Modern Era – A Complete Record	1-874287-33-3
Peterborough United: Who's Who?	1-874287-48-1
Plymouth Argyle: The Modern Era – A Complete Record	1-874287-54-6
Plymouth Argyle: 101 Golden Greats	1-874287-64-3
Plymouth Argyle: Snakes & Ladders – Promotions and Relegations	1-874287-82-1
Portsmouth: From Tindall to Ball – A Complete Record	1-874287-25-2
Portsmouth: Champions of England – 1948-49 & 1949-50	1-874287-38-4
The Story of the Rangers 1873-1923	1-874287-16-3
The Romance of the Wednesday 1867-1926	1-874287-17-1
Stoke City: The Modern Era – A Complete Record	1-874287-76-7
Stoke City: 101 Golden Greats	1-874287-55-4
Potters at War: Stoke City 1939-47	1-874287-78-3
Tottenham Hotspur: Champions of England 1950-51, 1960-61	1-874287-84-8
West Ham: From Greenwood to Redknapp	1-874287-19-8
West Ham: The Elite Era – A Complete Record	1-874287-31-7
Wimbledon: From Southern League to Premiership	1-874287-09-0
Wimbledon: From Wembley to Selhurst	1-874287-20-1
Wimbledon: The Premiership Years	1-874287-40-6
Wrexham: The European Era – A Complete Record	1-874287-52-X
WORLD CUP HISTORIES	
England's Quest for the World Cup – A Complete Record	1-874287-61-9
Scotland: The Quest for the World Cup – A Complete Record	1-897850-50-6
Ireland: The Quest for the World Cup – A Complete Record	1-897850-80-8
MISCELLANEOUS	
Red Dragons in Europe – A Complete Record	1-874287-01-5
The Book of Football: A History to 1905-06	1-874287-13-9
Football's War & Peace: The Tumultuous Season of 1946-47	1-874287-70-8

DUNDEE

Champions of Scotland 1961-62

Series Editor: Clive Leatherdale

Kenny Ross

DESERT ISLAND BOOKS

First Paperback Edition published in 2004
First Hardback Edition published in 2003
by
DESERT ISLAND BOOKS LIMITED
7 Clarence Road, Southend on Sea, Essex SS1 1AN
United Kingdom
www.desertislandbooks.com

British Library Cataloguing-in-Publication Data
A catalogue record for this book is available from the British Library

ISBN 1-874287-86-4

Printed in Great Britain
by
4Edge Ltd

Photographs in this book are reproduced by kind permission of:
DC Thomson

~ CONTENTS ~

~ Preface ~

Although it is now some 40 years since Dundee Football Club won the Scottish League Championship for the first and only time, that day at Muirton Park remains, without a shadow of doubt, the most memorable, wonderful day of my entire footballing career.

I will never forget the events of 28 April 1962, the pre-match trepidation, the after-match euphoria, the bus trip back to Dundee from Perth, the team's ecstatic reception on the balcony of Dundee Town Hall by the fans, the celebration dinner, and subsequently a somewhat hazy alcohol-fuelled recollection of the following few days. What a fantastic, unforgettable weekend!

Needless to say, these memories will remain with me for the rest of my life and I am eternally grateful to have been part of all the varying elements within the set-up at Dens Park. These all came together and culminated in the winning of the Championship and, the following year, our great run to the semi-final of the European Cup.

It was a pity to have had to leave such a set-up, but I had to try myself in what I considered a higher league, not to mention the obvious financial benefit. However, I believe that, had the Dundee team stayed essentially the same for a few years thereafter, even greater things might have been achieved.

Nevertheless, it was a great experience in my time to have been associated with Dundee Football Club and, even now, I think back fondly of my time there.

I am pleased therefore to have the opportunity to write the preface for this book, 'Dundee: Champions of Scotland', which charts those fantastic days and I wish it every success.

Ian Ure

~ Author's Note ~

I first went to watch Dundee when I was three years old when my father took me to see Dundee play St Johnstone at Muirton Park. It was the start of a love affair which has lasted every day since, supporting Dundee through the good times and bad. I was brought up on tales of the great Dundee sides from the 1950s and 60s, but they seemed almost unbelievable as we watched Dundee struggle constantly with financial crisis and relegation. Tales of Dundee's League triumph and subsequent European adventures always dominated the stories of the older fans, and a Dundee fanzine entitled 'Eh Mind O Gillie' even appeared in the 1990s.

Muirton Park, where Dundee enjoyed their finest hour, is now an ASDA superstore, with no plaque to commemorate what happened there on 28 April 1962. This book relives a tale of a time, and a triumph for a city, a football club, its players and its fans.

In writing this book, I am indebted to the many players, supporters and friends who gave their time, help and encouragement. In particular I would like to thank Alan Gilzean, Bobby Wishart, Bobby Cox, Bobby Seith, Bobby Waddell, Alan Cousin, and Ian Ure – who also wrote the preface. I would also like to thank fellow Dundee authors and friends, Jim Hendry and Norrie Price, fellow 'champions' authors Peter Rundo (Dundee United) and Kevin Stirling (Aberdeen) for putting me right on a few things, and Bob Crampsey for his insight into the time.

I am grateful to Dave Forbes at Dundee FC for his help and for giving me the chance to write for the Dundee match programme for the past seven years; and to David Young, Dundee FC's official website editor for his help, advice, and lifts back from midweek away games. Bob Donald, Alastair Strachan, Ron Hill, Jim Mitchell, Derek Burgess, Scott Glenday, Ian Glenday and Derek Cook were unstinting in their support. I would also like to thank Anne Swadel in the photo files at DC Thomson and Calum Laird in the DC Thomson Syndications Department. My friends and staff in my pub, The Golden Tee, also deserve a mention for their help, interest and encouragement, especially Carol Shirran and my assistant manager Liz Buchan who covered my shifts as deadlines were looming. It goes without saying that I would like to thank my Mum and my family for their encouragement and thank my best friend, Vicky McAuley, without whose help and encouragement, this book couldn't have been written.

My publisher and editor Clive Leatherdale deserves the biggest thanks for his guidance and for having the patience of a saint. His attention to detail and quality are inspiring, and I hope I didn't drive him too close to the brink.

But most of all, I want to thank my Dad, whom I miss so much and whom I hope is up there looking down very proud indeed. This book is dedicated to him for the love and support he gave to me and for introducing and sharing with me his passion for Dundee Football Club and his tales of Gillie & Co. I just hope that one day I will get the chance to write a sequel with tales to be told about new heroes and another Championship win. You can but dream!

KENNY ROSS

~ CHAMPIONS OF SCOTLAND ~

On Saturday, 28 April 1962, just before 4.20pm at Muirton Park in Perth, Dundee FC centre-forward Alan Cousin and St Johnstone centre-half Jim Ferguson chased a through ball into Saints' penalty-box. The defender reached it first but instead of clearing upfield he hit a weak effort straight to Hugh Robertson out on the Dundee left wing. Robertson squared the ball across the eighteen-yard line to 19-year-old Andy Penman, who crashed in an unstoppable shot via the crossbar past Bill Taylor in the Perth goal. That goal gave Dundee a 3-0 lead over their Tayside neighbours and, although there were still 23 minutes to play, it all but confirmed that Dundee would claim the Scottish League championship for the first and, to date, only time in their history. This was the top of the table before that climactic final match.

	P	W	D	L	F	A	Pts
Dundee	33	24	4	6	77	46	52
Rangers	33	22	6	5	83	30	50

Dundee needed just one point to see the League flag come to Dens. Local bookmakers were offering just 1:2 on for Dundee to win the title. Rangers, meanwhile, sat two points behind but with a vastly superior goal average of 2.76 compared to Dundee's 1.67. Goal average was an archaic method of separating teams level on points until replaced by goal difference in the 1970s. It meant dividing the number of goals scored by the number conceded, and required in those pre-calculator days a working knowledge of long division. Rangers were at home to Kilmarnock and faced odds of 3:1 to retain their title. The bookies therefore looked to be backing Dundee.

As for St Johnstone, this was also a critical fixture. They needed one point to guarantee their safety and avoid relegation. The Saints were sitting fourteenth pre-match, in an eighteen-club league, two places above the trap-door. They had the same points as Raith Rovers but with a worse goal average. With Stirling Albion already relegated, the Saints were still a point ahead of Falkirk and two ahead of Airdrie and St Mirren. In short, St Johnstone could afford to drop two places, but not three.

	P	W	D	L	F	A	Pts
Raith	33	9	7	17	48	72	25
St Johnstone	33	9	7	17	35	58	25
Falkirk	33	10	4	19	43	68	24
Airdrie	33	8	7	18	56	77	23
St Mirren	33	9	5	19	48	79	23
Stirling	33	6	6	21	33	73	18

St Johnstone could take nothing for granted. Raith, Falkirk, Airdrie and St Mirren were also all playing at home. They might all pick up points and send St Johnstone plummeting into the Second Division.

With both Dundee and their opponents needing only a draw to achieve their respective targets, human nature might have suggested a have-as-we-hold stalemate. Not exactly a fix, but a safety-first non-event, with players giving sideways passes to wind down the clock. There are plenty of clubs who might have resorted to this, but for Dundee that was never an option in the eyes of the players or the fans. Thirteen years earlier, Dundee's title hopes disappeared on the last day, at Brockville, when a draw was all they needed. Dundee manager Bob Shankly had witnessed that disaster – as boss of Falkirk – and wanted no repetition.

Dundee were on a roll with six wins on the trot and the players were keen to extend this to 'lucky seven'. There is also the delicate matter of alleged bribery. In his autobiography, *Ure's Truly*, centre-half Ian Ure tells of a message passed to the Dundee players in the dressing room before kick-off. They stood to collect £50 each – a sizeable sum in 1962 – if they 'arranged' matters to allow the game to end all-square. Bribery at this time was rife within the British game. Ure, however, states that the offer, from an unknown source, was treated with contempt. In fact, it only served to double Dundee's determination. If St Johnstone wanted their point to guarantee safety, they would have to earn it fair and square.

Twenty thousand Dundonians formed the bulk of the 26,500 crowd. It was a gloriously sunny day, with many of the crowd in short sleeves. With tension mounting, ambulance men were kept busy from an hour before the game with dozens of fainting cases to deal with.

At 2.55pm the teams came out to an explosion of noise that Muirton Park had probably never before experienced. St Johnstone ran out first in their change strip of all white (the practice in Scotland was for the home team to change if necessary, so that the travelling party only had to carry one set of kit), but when Dundee emerged in their traditional V-neck dark blue shirts, white shorts and blue socks, the noise from Dundee larynxes and whirling rattles dwarfed the Perth welcome.

The Perth side included young Alex Ferguson, who would later manage Aberdeen and Manchester United. The 20-year-old Ferguson lined up at inside-left: he only switched to centre-forward after his transfer to Rangers. He was an important component in a Perth side who hadn't defeated Dundee since 1937.

On a bone-hard pitch, Dundee survived a scare when Alex Hamilton cleared Ferguson's header off the line, but the destiny of the title tilted Dundee's way after 24 minutes. Veteran Gordon Smith, 38 years old and on the verge of winning his fifth league championship with his third club, hit a swirling cross into the Saints' box, where Alan Gilzean headed the ball into the net. The huge travelling support erupted.

A few of the crowd carried battery powered radios and were aware of developments at other grounds. At half-time there was contrasting news for supporters of Dundee and St Johnstone. At Ibrox, Rangers were being held 1-1 by fifth-placed Kilmarnock, who had equalised an early Rangers strike. For St Johnstone, the grim news was that that two of the three teams immediately below them were winning. Falkirk were leading Third Lanark 1-0, while St Mirren were beating Jock Stein's Dunfermline 2-1. Airdrie were locked goalless with Partick. It was, therefore, dangerously uncomfortable for Dundee's opponents.

Traditionally, in the days before crowd segregation, supporters would change ends during the ten-minute break and converge behind the goal into which their team would be attacking. However, with a capacity crowd at Muirton, and Dundee fans wedged behind both goals, most spectators stayed where they were.

Dundee's nerves were eased in the 59th minute when Gilzean notched his second goal of the game and his 27th of the season. Full-back Alex Hamilton sent a long ball through the middle for 'Gillie' to nod it past Saints' Jim Ferguson and score past Taylor at the second attempt.

Many Dundee fans switched off their radios at this point as the result at Ibrox was academic. But for St Johnstone the news had gotten worse. Airdrie were now one up against seventh-placed Thistle, while Falkirk and St Mirren had two-goal leads. If matters stayed as they were, the Saints would go down.

St Johnstone's agony was complete and their fate sealed in the final minutes. Having now gone three goals behind, Alex Ferguson had a header ruled out for fouling Ian Ure, whom he had climbed all over in the process of 'scoring'. Ferguson's goal would have made the score 3-1, but his effort might have been no mere consolation. It could have been the difference between staying up and going down, although in the event St Johnstone's goal average was still worse than St Mirren's.

When the final whistle sounded just after 4.40pm to cement Dundee's 3-0 win, thousands of supporters, young and old, rained onto the pitch in a human tidal wave to congratulate their heroes and hail the new 'Champions of Scotland'.

Rangers had drawn 1-1, leaving Dundee with a three-point gap at the top. But for St Johnstone it was heartbreak. Airdrie had won 1-0, Falkirk had finished 2-0, St Mirren 4-1 against the Pars, and Raith had beaten Aberdeen 3-1. The four teams around them, in other words, had all won, and that extraordinarily improbable scenario meant that St Johnstone had dipped into the bottom two – relegated on goal average.

But for Dundee it was nothing but joy. Several players were carried off shoulder high by delirious fans. Shankly ran onto the park at the final whistle to congratulate his team but wisely had second thoughts when he was engulfed by Dundee supporters. The players had their backs slapped, hands shaken, and those that weren't carried off, like Gilzean, had to fight their way through the crowd with police assistance to get to the sanctuary of the dressing room.

The supporters demanded that their heroes reappear to take a bow, even though the championship trophy was not there to be paraded. In those days it was the custom to hand it over to the winning club, without ceremony, at a later date. But that did not stop the Dark Blue faithful clamouring for another sight of the champions.

'The team will not appear,' came the announcement, but seconds later a mighty roar went up as skipper Bobby Cox led his players up into the main stand to acknowledge the fans. It was a moment that seemed to last for ever; a dream come true, that no one in their wildest fantasies could have predicted nine months previously. For those who had witnessed Dundee's 1-4 defeat to Falkirk in 1949, allowing Rangers to snatch the league title, the pain of that moment was now momentarily erased.

After emerging from the dressing room the players were blockaded in the car park, and it took an age for them and Dundee's officials to board the team coach.

The 25-mile journey back to Dundee was equally slow. The road from the Fair City of Perth was head to tail with motor cars bedecked with dark blue scarves swinging from their windows. Nobody cared how long the journey took, especially those on the team bus, where the players were led in their singing by Ian Ure. The ecstatic fans gave the team bus a noisy escort back from Perth and, when it arrived back in Dundee, thousands lined the streets.

The Dundee party headed for the city square, where thousands more had gathered, then into the City Council Chambers to appear on the balcony and accept yet more adulation. The players were greeted by Dundee Lord Provost McManus and by Dundee MP Morgan Thomson, and as the champagne corks popped, slurred speeches were uttered and yet more handshakes proferred.

Later, players and officials congregated at chairman James Gellatly's house in Broughty Ferry for yet more drinks before assembling in a city hotel for a meal. The celebrations had only really begun, for the city had not seen anything like this since VE Day. Many pubs stayed open beyond their licensing hours of 10 or perhaps 11pm, but nobody cared.

It had been a tremendous climax to an unforgettable season which is still talked about today by those who were there to witness Dundee's remarkable achievement. After starting the season with a nineteen-game unbeaten run, it looked like the team might blow their chances with an alarming winter slump which allowed Rangers to claw back an eight-point lead. However, after Rangers had gone top of the league, Dundee halted a run of four defeats by holding the Gers to a scoreless draw at Dens. They then won their last seven games to clinch the championship. The run was made all the more remarkable by the fact that five of those last seven games had been away from home, one of which was at Tannadice on Easter Monday.

All season the Dark Blues had displayed the ability to win the league but they also showed a fighting spirit that the press insisted they didn't have. In several games Dundee came storming back to win when all had looked lost, and that spirit undoubtedly carried them through in the final run home.

Success was also helped by a consistency of selection. Remarkably, Dundee called upon only fifteen players the whole season. Admittedly, the club were lucky with injuries and enjoyed a period where few if any players suffered a prolonged loss of form. Early in the season a recognised first eleven quickly established themselves. The names of those favoured eleven became immortalised for future generations thanks to a reworking of the song 'Bonnie Dundee', sung by Hector Nicol. It greeted the Dundee team running out at Dens for over 30 years.

'We've got Robertson, Penman and Alan Gilzean,
With Cousin and Smith, they're the finest you've seen,
A defence that is steady, heroic and sure,
Liney, Hamilton, Cox, Seith, and Wishart and Ure'

Those who saw that great team, however, don't need that last verse of that song to recall the names. Dundee were fortunate to have the calibre of players like Craig Brown, George McGeachie, Alec Stuart and Bobby Waddell to deputise when necessary eighteen times between them.

Five of the squad – Alan Gilzean, Gordon Smith, Bobby Cox, Bobby Seith and Bobby Waddell – hailed from the general Tayside and Dundee area and, compared to today's modern cosmopolitan football, this constitutes a high percentage of local talent. For example, Dundee's sixteen-man squad stripped for the 2003 Scottish Cup final could boast of only one Dundee-born player – substitute Steven Milne.

The title-winning Dundee side are immortalised at Dens Park today with hospitality lounges named after Andy Penman and Alex Hamilton. An even greater acknowledgement came when the Dundee fans voted in 1999 to name the two new Dens Park stands after the captain and manager who led Dundee to the heights.

Captain Bobby Cox is still a regular at Dens, chatting to those who attend the hospitality. He can often be found on matchdays in the club shop, adjacent to the home stand that bears his name. Cox was a key figure in the title success and was described by Shankly's right-hand man, trainer Sammy Kean, as a 'real tiger, a born winner who never gave up and whose influence was immense'.

Cox was the left-back in the side and with right-back Alex Hamilton combined to be arguably the best two full-backs in Scotland at the time. At 5ft 7in, Cox was a small but mighty defender. A rugged Dundonian, born and bred a few hundred yards from Dens Park in Wedderburn Street, he joined the Dark Blues from local side Osbourne in 1956. He started off as an inside-forward and then moved to wing-half before the Army changed him into a full-back during his National Service – much to the fortune of Dundee a few years later.

Cox missed only three games in the 1961-62 campaign and eventually notched up a total of 411 appearances for Dundee in all competitions between 1956 and 1969. He has made the third most appearances for Dundee, behind Doug Cowie and Bill Marsh, and was unfortunate not to be capped for Scotland at any level, despite the press and the match programmes at the time touting him to appear for Scotland. Sadly for Cox, Eric Caldow of Rangers was automatic first choice for the national side and, while being no better a footballer than Cox, Caldow was perhaps more accomplished on the ball and took responsibilities for penalty-kicks as well. For Cox not to have earned even an Under-23, Under-21 or Scottish League cap, however, is surprising to anyone who saw him play. Even after Caldow broke his leg, it was Provan and Kennedy of Celtic who replaced him and Cox had to be content with being on the international reserve list.

The current away stand at Dens bears the name of the man who managed the team to their unique triumph. Bob Shankly was a quiet, rather unassuming man away from football, who was spotted mowing the lawn in his garden early on the Sunday morning the day after Dundee were crowned champions.

Dundee's previous manager, Willie Thornton, bequeathed some of Scotland's brightest young stars when he departed in 1959, but Shankly had to nurture their talents to the full and brought in experienced men like Bobby Seith, Bobby Wishart and Gordon Smith to produce a ripe blend of youth and experience.

Smith, in particular, became a vital cog in the Dundee championship wheel and, while he was no longer blessed with the pace of old, he was invaluable in bringing out the best in the young forwards – Cousin, Penman and Gilzean – with whom he at times appeared to have a telepathic understanding.

Shankly, along with his backroom team of Sammy Kean, Lawrie Smith and Jacky Kay, moulded Dundee into what Scottish football historian Bob Crampsey describes as the 'best pure footballing team produced in Scotland since the war'.

The team had skill, enthusiasm and running power, which they combined with great effect with a fast, flowing and incisive passing game from front to back. Jim Hendry, author of *Dundee Greats*, likened the team to a machine, with essential parts all moving in unison to produce a Rolls Royce, 'A sleek, prowling, all powerful piece of work, polished by Bob Shankly until it gleamed with pride and moved into football's fast lane.'

The Dundee champions could play football all right, but they were also great friends off the park, especially the crop of youngsters who had come through the reserves together. They wanted to work together and work hard for each other and the work paid off.

Success was a new experience, however, not just for the majority of the players, but also for the city of Dundee and its success-starved public. Dundee Football Club was taking its followers to heights never visited before, not just domestically, but also on the famous European adventure the following year.

The 1960s was a turbulent decade that saw several revolutions – socially, politically, militarily and musically – but the revolution that first captured the interest and hearts around the River Tay was the one led by Gillie, Shanks, Bobby Cox and Co.

This is the story of Dundee: Champions of Scotland.

Chapter 1

~ Foundations ~

(1944 – 1954)

When Scottish League football was suspended on 3 September 1939, due to the outbreak of the Second World War, Dundee FC had plummeted to its lowest position in its 46-year history. Despite sitting top of the Scottish League Division Two with maximum points after four games, the future of Dundee FC did not look bright. The club had failed to win promotion the previous season in what was their first ever outside the top division.

Dundee had been relegated for the first time at the end of 1937-38 and had been expected to bounce back immediately. Despite, however, reputedly having the richest directorate in Scottish Football, in the guise of 'Jute Barons' Simpson, Graham, How and Galloway, they failed to make an impact and finished off the pace in sixth.

Gates at Dens Park had also hit an all-time low, with a paltry 1,700 present to witness the last home game of the season, against Dumbarton in April. By the time the new season arrived, pessimism was rampant. Mind you, events at Dens were paling into insignificance compared to those on the world stage.

Just 2,000 fans turned out at Broomfield to see Dundee defeat Airdrie on 19 August, but when it was announced two days later that Hitler and Stalin had signed a non-aggression pact, it did not stop the Government preparing for war. In Dundee, children were evacuated, in the main to the rural area of Kincardineshire between Dundee and Aberdeen. Air-raid shelters were constructed and gas masks acquired.

Dundee did give their fans something to cheer about on 30 August, when they defeated Dundee United 6-1 in the Forfarshire Cup, but two days later Hitler invaded Poland, and Britain and France responded with a declaration of war.

Although the Scottish League suspended its competition immediately, it soon became clear that football would help sustain the morale of the nation and by October new regional leagues were formed. Crowds were limited to 8,000 for fear of German air-raid attacks. Dundee entered into the new Eastern Division but still continued to struggle as players volunteered for service or were called up. With an average crowd of just 3,000 and a £1,400 financial loss for the season, Dundee decided in May 1940 to close for the duration. Dens Park was used by the Decontamination (Food) Service until football resumed four years later.

That break was vital for the restructuring and future of Dundee FC. Directors William Hood, Robert Paterson and James Meechan retired and vice-chairman David How died. The shares of How and Simpson were purchased by a local consortium. At the club's AGM in April 1944 a new board was elected, with consortium members John Thomson, James Gellatly, Murray Wilkie, Jack Swadel and – most significantly – George Anderson co-opted onto the board. With the tide of war turning in the Allies' favour, preparations began in August 1944 for Dundee to resume playing football. George Anderson was placed in charge of team affairs.

Anderson had been a director of his hometown club, Aberdeen. He had been put in charge of team matters at Pittodrie in 1939, when manager Davie Halliday went off to war. Anderson revelled in the position of caretaker manager but as it was being held for the return of Halliday, Anderson made a move for the position at Dens. He had guested for Dundee during the First World War and now used his many contacts to build a new team. When Dundee returned to play in the Scottish North-East Division in October 1944, the team contained only two players to have played in the final game four years earlier.

On 5 August 1944, two months after the D-day landings, Dundee returned to action against the British Army, in effect an almost entirely international eleven, which included Matt Busby, Joe Mercer and Frank Swift. Despite the Dees going down 0-7, Busby complimented their 'cultured style of play'. A week later Dundee opened their league campaign in Kirkcaldy against Raith Rovers.

Dundee won the North-East Division in 1944-45 and the Scottish 'B' Division the season after, but the club had to wait until it won a third 'championship' in a row in 1946-47 before it was granted promotion. Due to the large number of guest players used by clubs and the number of players still being demobbed, the Scottish League had decided not to re-insert promotion or relegation until 1947. After ten years out of the top flight, the Dark Blues were back in the big time for the start of the 1947-48 campaign and Anderson was the toast of the city.

Anderson, known affectionately by the players as Toffee Dod because of the confectionery business he owned in Aberdeen, showed himself to be a forward planner and a progressive football thinker. He had constantly been gearing Dundee for life in the top flight and had been signing players with the 'A' Division in mind. Amongst those signings were future captain Alfie Boyd, Doug Cowie (who holds the record number of appearances for the club), and Tommy Gallacher (son of Patsy, uncle of Kevin, who would write for the Dundee *Courier* upon retiring from the game). Gallacher had turned out for Dundee during the War. Anderson also recruited English centre-forward Albert Juliussen, who would write his name into the history books at Dens Park.

On consecutive Saturdays, Juliussen scored 'double' hat-tricks when he scored six goals at Alloa in March 1947 and seven a week later at home to Dunfermline, as Dundee racked up two 10-0 victories. The wins still, to this day, constitute Dundee's highest ever victories.

Anderson was a master of man-management and popular with the players with his emphasis on ball-work in training. He excelled in public relations and attempted to raise the profile of the club. He also had an eye for talent and had constructed a skilful, attractive side in a relatively short space of time. So much so, that they were ready for an assault on Scotland's elite.

Anderson still lived in Aberdeen, where he was a town councillor and from where he ran his confectionery business. He travelled down to Dundee twice a week. The day-to-day training was left to assistants Willie Cameron and Andy McCall, but the bowler-hatted, bow-tied, larger-than-life Anderson had the full support and respect of the players, despite his infrequent appearances at the club.

It is said that Anderson would tell the players to 'go out and enjoy themselves' on a Saturday afternoon. He liked to encourage attractive football and Dundee's first season back in the top flight was rewarded with a fourth-place finish in a sixteen-team league, their highest placing for 26 years.

Dundee were ready, therefore, for an assault on the championship. Anderson announced pre-season that his players were not for sale and that young talent would be encouraged to blossom. The club practised exactly what Anderson preached. Of Dundee's 32-man squad in 1948, twenty had been signed from juveniles or juniors, and several had been recruited from local clubs. Anderson also signed players from his home base in Aberdeen. Among them were Doug Cowie, Syd Gerrie and young forward George Christie, whom he spotted playing for Banks O'Dee juniors and to whom he gave a job in his Aberdeen sweet factory.

Dundee had served notice of their intent on the last day of 1947-48, when they recorded a 3-1 home win over already-crowned champions Hibernian. By November the following season they lay second, just two points behind the Easter Road side, and had won through to a Scottish League Cup semi-final against Rangers.

The League Cup was still in its infancy. The idea emerged during the War, when the SFA suspended the Scottish Cup. Those League clubs still in action began competing for their own knock-out trophy. When league football resumed, it was decided to retain a league cup competition and contest it from the start of each season. Dundee's semi-final against Rangers was played in appalling conditions at Hampden with a gale-force wind and torrential rain. Rangers won the toss and opted to play with the conditions in their favour in the first half. Having lost the choice of ends, Dundee should have been allowed to kick-off, but apparently the referee allowed Rangers to do so, and within a minute of the start the Gers had taken the lead.

Dundee lost defender Tommy Gray, injured during the first goal, and within seven minutes the Dees were three down. Referee Livingstone would later receive a reprimand, but it was little consolation for Dundee who eventually lost 1-4, with a second-half consolation penalty from Reggie Smith.

Disappointment was short-lived. By the time Rangers came to Dens on 3 January, Dundee lay just one point behind the Ibrox team in second place. Dundee considered themselves unfortunate not to be level on points, as Third Lanark's Polish winger Staroscik had fisted the ball into the Dundee net in the last minute to give the Hi-His a draw three weeks earlier. A win now would put Dundee top for the first time.

The official crowd was 39,975 but it was estimated that there was another 6,000 inside and another 5,000 on the streets outside. Perhaps the club were fortunate to escape a Hillsborough-style disaster. As for the game, Marshall's early goal for Rangers was countered by Ernie Ewan's thunderbolt and two goals from Alec Stott.

Dundee stayed top of the league for several months. They also progressed to the Scottish Cup semi-final, where they faced Clyde, whom they had beaten to lift the trophy for the only time in 1910. Despite losing to the Shawfield club in a replay, dashing their hopes of a double, Dundee were still favourites to win the championship.

On the penultimate day of the season Dundee defeated struggling Motherwell 2-1 at Dens in front of 26,000 fans, and Rangers won 1-0 at Morton. Dundee had retained their one-point lead over the Ibrox side, which meant that a win in their final game at Falkirk would guarantee the title, irrespective of Rangers' result at Albion Rovers.

On Saturday, 30 April 1949, 17,000 crammed into Falkirk's sun-kissed Brockville stadium but the thousands who had travelled from Dundee were blissfully unaware of the nerves flooding through their heroes in the dressing room. The normally effervescent and chirpy Anderson was unable to dispel them. When confronted with the usual pre-match opposition banter, Anderson locked his troops in the dressing room an hour before kick off.

The tension built to such an intensity that by the time Dundee took to the field they looked thoroughly unnerved and gave the impression that they might freeze. It was an error of judgment by Anderson who, in trying to protect his players from unnecessary distractions, now had to sit back helplessly as his team fell apart.

Managed by Bob Shankly, mid-table Falkirk had little to play for. Just before half-time Dundee were awarded a penalty when George 'Pud' Hill was brought down in the box. Alec Stott, Scotland's leading goalscorer, had assumed Dundee's spot-kick duties from Pattillo, following the latter's miss at Love Street. Stott's own record with penalties was flawless but he failed to make clean contact with the ball and George Nicol in the Bairns' goal dived to his right to turn it round the post.

At half-time Dundee learned that Rangers were two up at Coatbridge, and within eight minutes of the restart Dundee were two down to Falkirk. Stott pulled one back before Falkirk bagged another two goals. The final score was 4-1 at both Brockville and Albion, but Dundee had lost and Rangers had won to claim the Scottish League championship for the 26th time. They had also wrested their crown back after Hibs had usurped the title the previous season. For Dundee it was heartbreak. The season had ended with two cup semi-final defeats and a runners-up spot in the league.

In just five short years, however, George Anderson had taken Dundee from Division Two also-rans to championship contenders. Despite coming so close to winning a haul of trophies, the facts showed that Dundee had still won nothing except their solitary Scottish Cup victory. A massive psychological block had to be overcome.

Anderson was beginning to transform Dundee into a cosmopolitan crew, signing various Englishmen, two South Africans (Gordon Frew and Ken Ziesing), a Canadian (Jack Cowan) and several Scandinavians who came and went. Anderson also signed Scottish inside-forward Bobby Flavell from Hearts and a promising 17-year-old goalkeeper, Bill Brown, from Carnoustie Panmure. The Scots in the side combined well with the imports, and Anderson relied particularly on the strong half-back line of Gallacher, Cowie and Boyd.

With James Gellatly installed as chairman, Anderson had a largely free hand in his transfer dealings. After seeing his team finish sixth in 1949-50, having fallen away after Christmas, Anderson knew he was still a player or two away from mounting another sustained challenge. If ever a transfer confirmed how far Anderson had taken Dundee, it was the buy he made in September 1950, one of the transfer coups of the century.

That player was Billy Steel, signed for what appears to have constituted a world record fee of £23,500. So huge was it that it was not surpassed in Scottish terms for over a decade, when George McLean signed for Rangers from St Mirren.

Steel was a footballing legend, the George Best, the Paul Gascoigne, the David Beckham of his time. He was a headline-maker, scandal-maker, a pin-up boy, but most of all he was a fabulous footballer who brought power, skill and imagination to Dundee's front line. The fee paid for him was extraordinary for its time, and for a provincial club like Dundee to land a player of Steel's calibre shocked the football world. He is, in the opinion of this author, Dundee's greatest ever signing, rivalled only by that of Claudio Caniggia half a century later.

At 26, Steel was already an established international. He had starred in Great Britain's 6-1 win over the Rest of Europe in 1947 and scored for Scotland in their 3-1 win over England at Wembley in 1949. His dazzling 1947 Scotland debut in a 1-1 Wembley draw prompted Derby County to pay Morton a then world record fee of £15,500 for the little inside-forward. The world seemed to be at the Dunipace man's feet.

Steel had demanded a house and a job outside of football before agreeing to sign, but he and his wife were slow to settle in Derby and the pressure of being the world's costliest player began to take its toll. Steel therefore informed his club that he would live in Scotland and travel to Derby on match-days. That arrangement was never going to work. In the summer of 1950, Steel took the unprecedented step of holding his own press conference in Glasgow, proclaiming that either he moved back to Scotland or he would quit the game. It was then that Anderson started to visualise Steel in the Dark Blue of Dundee.

Anderson's initial offer of £18,000 was rebuffed. Steel accepted training facilities with Rangers and looked for a while to be heading for Govan but Rangers manager Bill Struth issued a statement that the Ibrox club would not be signing Billy Steel.

When Anderson returned from a secret trip to Derby he called his own press conference and to the astonishment of the pressmen in attendance announced 'Gentleman, I want to introduce you to Billy Steel, ex-Derby County and now of Dundee'.

It was a huge gamble for the club, not only in financial terms, but also because of Steel's personality. He was volatile, sharp as a tack, and his own team-mates were as likely to be on the end of a verbal volley as the opposition. He was not lacking in confidence, however, and when asked what it was like to be a £23,500 player he replied: 'Nothing to it. When I left Morton I needed a suitcase to carry my share.'

Fears that Steel might not make an impact at Dens were blown away on his debut on 23 September 1950, when 34,000 turned up against Aberdeen – 10,000 more than had been expected. With admission prices ranging from one shilling and sixpence (7½p) to five shillings (25p), Steel had at a stroke chalked £4,000 off his transfer fee. He delighted the huge crowd with a virtuoso display and the first goal in a 2-0 win.

In December, the club's highest league crowd of the season (home or away), 37,400, saw a 2-0 win over leaders Rangers, with Dundee wearing continental style rubber boots. Anderson had acquired them to help his players keep their feet on the frosty, sanded pitch. It is thought that Dundee were the first team in Scotland to wear such footwear.

By early March, Dundee lay just two points behind leaders Hibs and had reached the Scottish Cup quarter-finals. A 1-2 defeat by Raith Rovers ended that Hampden trail, and league defeats by East Fife and Airdrie put paid to title hopes for another season. Dundee finished third, ten points behind champions Hibs. But Dundee only had a few months to wait to get their hands around a cup.

Pre-season press chatter saw one local paper describe Dundee as a side 'with the potential to win the Scottish Cup'. In many ways the Cup to football fans was far more important than the League. It provided a greater sense of occasion and, at a time when few fans followed their team away, going 'Up for the Cup' still exerted a powerful hold. A potential trip to a Hampden final held a special appeal.

This was only logical. The Cup was for many clubs the 'holy grail'. The prospect of winning the championship was remote for most, fewer teams got relegated in those days and, in any case, the financial repercussions for doing so were less severe than they are now. There were no European places at stake, and no pressure to finish in the top six. In other words, for most clubs there was nothing to play for from one month to the next – except in the Cup. In fact, Anderson was ahead of his time, somewhat, regularly calling for a smaller league where the matches would be more meaningful.

Crowds for League Cup-ties, it is surprising to learn, were also higher than for league matches between the same opposition. The 1951-52 season started with Dundee in the same section as three other 'A' Division sides – St Mirren, Hearts and Raith Rovers. Only the group winners qualified, and Dundee squeezed through, courtesy of a last gasp win at Raith.

The quarter-final paired the Dark Blues with 'B' Division Falkirk, and Dundee escaped from Brockville with a 0-0 draw in the first leg. At Dens,

Falkirk scored first, but were finally beaten by goals from Steel and Ziesing. The other semi-finalists were Rangers, Celtic and Motherwell. The draw was kind, pitting Dundee with the Fir Park side at Ibrox. Steel set up four of his side's five goals, his new strike partner, Bobby Flavell, grabbing a hat-trick.

On 22 October 1951 Dundee faced up to Rangers in their first post-War final, and 30,000 Dundonians clogged the roads to the national stadium and congregated mainly under the old north stand.

Rangers captain George Young won the toss and chose to attack the traditional Rangers end. Dundee had played towards the Rangers end in the first half of their two losing semis in 1948-49, and so were happy to be kicking the other way. Not that it appeared to have made much difference because, playing in white, Dundee fell behind to a Findlay goal.

Anderson changed tactics at half-time, adopting a short-passing game to draw out the Rangers defence. Goals by Flavell and Johnny 'Straight-back' Pattillo turned the tables, but with two minutes left a free-kick by Rangers' skipper George Young was bundled in by Willie Thornton. The 92,235 crowd were spared extra-time when Steel floated a free-kick to Alfie Boyd at the far post. The ball flew into the Rangers net to give Dundee the prize of which they had dreamed.

The Dundee party had travelled to Glasgow by train and when they returned to Dundee's West Station they found huge crowds there to greet them. By a quirk of fate, the policeman on duty at the station was a Mr James Goldie of Lochee who had also policed Dundee's triumphant return from Ibrox 42 years earlier in 1910. At Yeoman Shore an open top bus was waiting take the players on a tour of the city centre. Thousands lined the streets and traffic was halted before the players headed off to Chairman Gellatly's house for a champagne reception.

George Anderson's hard work and vision, not least in signing Billy Steel, appeared to have paid off. Winning a major trophy as early as October can easily backfire, however, and before long Dundee had spiralled towards the relegation zone. It was the arrival of the Scottish Cup that kick-started the season into life. Ayr United, non-league Wigtown, and 'C' Division Berwick Rangers were all overcome to propel Dundee into semi-finals devoid of the Old Firm. In these circumstances, Dundee, Hearts, Motherwell and Third Lanark all fancied their chances.

Dundee took on Third Lanark at Easter Road. Steel had been plagued by an ankle injury and opted out of the Scotland v England international in order to try to be fit for the semi-final. Dundee had reason to be grateful that he did, for Steel made the first goal and scored the second in a 2-0 win.

That meant Dundee were booked for their second Hampden cup final in six months. They started favourites against Motherwell, despite finishing below them in the league. The gates closed ten minutes before kick-off, shutting out 1,000 Dundee fans whose football special train had been delayed. The crowd was given as 136,274, the second largest in Scottish Cup final history, exceeded only by the 147,365 which attended Aberdeen v Celtic in 1937.

Dundee were unable to strike gold a second time. Motherwell fired four second-half goals without reply to lift the trophy for the first time. On the Monday, the *Courier* cartoonist John Mason joked that Dundee fans would have to listen to the old timers harping on about the 1910 win, but two Hampden appearances in quick succession suggested that Dundee had arrived as a footballing force. They quickly made it three, retaining the League Cup by beating 'B' Division Kilmarnock 2-0 in October 1953. Nine football specials conveyed 5,000 Dundee fans to Hampden, a similar number travelled by coach, and countless others made their own way. Anderson himself would not be there, being taken ill with pleurisy and listening to the game on the radio in his Aberdeen nursing home. He would have been cheered by news of Bobby Flavell's two late goals, which meant Dundee were the first side to successfully defend the Scottish League Cup. The players returned to Dundee to be greeted by fireworks, whistles and bugles when their train pulled in to Dundee West at 8.35pm.

Once again, a large crowd had assembled in the city square but the players' open top bus took a different route from last time and headed for the chairman's house in West Ferry, via Victoria Road. Mr Gellatly hosted a small party in Albany Road before the players and officials headed back into town for a meal in the Royal British Hotel.

These were heady days for football attendances. Dundee's average league gate that season when Billy Steel arrived was 23,500. Compare that with the season that Claudio Caniggia graced Dens Park, when only 7,200 turned up to watch his debut. When the Scottish Cup came around in early 1953, Rangers' visit smashed the Dens attendance record, though the 43,024 spectators inside the ground saw the Gers deny Dundee a unique 'double, double' cup final appearance. The current capacity at Dens is 12,200, so the record set in February 1953 – three and a half times the current capacity – will never be broken.

At the end of that season Dundee were snubbed by the football authorities, who declined to invite the Dark Blues to participate in the Coronation Cup, to celebrate the accession of Queen Elizabeth II. Four clubs from England – Arsenal, Manchester United, Newcastle United and Tottenham – joined four from Scotland – Celtic, Rangers, Hibs and Aberdeen. Rangers had won the league and Scottish Cup, while Hibs and Aberdeen had been invited as runners-up in both. Dundee felt aggrieved because they had won back-to-back League Cups and finished higher in the league than Celtic and Aberdeen. In the event, the tournament was won by Celtic.

Instead of taking the huff, Dundee contended themselves with a summer tour to South Africa, organised by the flamboyant Anderson to assist the SFA, which found itself unable to fulfil a commitment it had already made. Considering their snub received in the Coronation Cup fiasco, it was a conciliatory gesture by Anderson, but he was always a master of both diplomacy and publicity. So much so, that Anderson made Dundee wear a tartan strip on the tour to emphasise that they were representing not just Dundee but Scotland too. The local newspaper headline after the first match read 'Tartan Troops from Tayside'. The tartan they wore? Anderson of course!

Dundee made a fine impression in South Africa, losing just one game in the punishing seventeen-match schedule. The tour included four 'test matches' against the South African national side, of which Dundee won three and lost one. They attended numerous Scottish Society functions across the country, but right-back Gerry Follon missed out. Follon was a schoolteacher in Dundee. It was decided by the local authority to prohibit Follon from travelling with the Dundee party because schoolteachers were in short supply.

But the Anderson era was nearing its end. His successful team began to break up and Anderson's health worsened during the summer of 1954. By then, Dundee had lost the Canadian Jack Cowan and South Africans Ken Ziesing and Gordon Frew, who all returned home, and Bobby Flavell, who was keen to try his luck in South Africa. Influential skipper Alfie Boyd remained in South Africa at the end of the tour to take up a coaching post, and when Dundee were knocked out of the Scottish Cup by 'C' Division Berwick, Anderson probably felt that he had perhaps taken Dundee as far as he could

Billy Steel's days at Dens were also numbered, despite his being made captain upon Boyd's departure. But that was a promotion doomed to failure. Steel's intolerance began to be resented by his team-mates. There had also been serious concerns that Steel's persistent ankle injury might terminate his career. For most of 1953-54 he was taking painkillers in an attempt to avoid surgery.

It soon became apparent to Anderson that Steel was not training in Glasgow as regularly as he claimed, and when the club gave Steel an ultimatum – train full-time at Dens or else – the player refused and was put up for sale.

No club was willing to take a risk on 31-year-old Steel, however, and, after three months without any offers coming in, he announced that he was moving to America to make a new life in California. He took up the job of manager of the Los Angeles Danes.

'Budgem', as Steel's team-mates called him, was gone and so too was George Anderson who retired in 1954 on account of his failing health. Dundee's golden post-War age was over, but Anderson had done much to lay the foundations of Dundee Football Club as a prominent force in Scottish football. He had won more trophies for the club than any other manager since its formation in 1893 although, with Dundee finishing seventh or eighth four seasons in a row, the club were clearly seen as cup specialists. Nevertheless, Anderson had seen his dream of a successful Dundee FC come true and had raised the profile and stature of the club beyond what had been before the War. His legacy was set and the foundations were in place to take Dundee to the next level.

Chapter 2

~ Change and Team-Building ~

(1954 – 1961)

Post-War Dundee had always been a vibrant city, but by the late 1950s it was changing out of all recognition. Modernisation had begun to transform the landscape, not only in the centre but also in the north, in the shape of new housing schemes known as 'avenues of hope'.

Dundee was, and is, a beautiful city built around the rock of an extinct volcano known locally as The Law. When approaching the city by train from Fife across the longest rail bridge in Europe, the magnificence of Dundee can be glimpsed. Dundonians returning home from the south often get goose bumps at the site of the city as it stretches along the Tay's estuary from Broughty Ferry in the east to Invergowrie in the west.

Some say that Dundee has a face that 'only a mother would love' but Dundonians are fiercely proud of their heritage. Other observers have described it as 'dour, grey or dull' but for those that come from it or have spent any time in it, this couldn't be further from the truth. The view from the top of The Law is spectacular and the stories that exist within this visual feast are rich and warm.

The promontory of Broughty Ferry, the rail and road bridges which pull together the green hills of Fife, the Sidlaws to the north, Balgay Hill to the west, and the hinterland of Perthshire which can be spied across the Tay Valley are among the views that give Dundee its flavour. There is also Lochee and the famous Cox's Stack tower, a testament to the importance to the city of jute, to the north-west. Then there is the Hilltown and the city centre to the south, while to the north-east, partially obscured by two of Dundee's many multi-story high-rise flats, are located Dens Park and Tannadice, home to the city's two football clubs, Dundee FC and Dundee United.

Dens and Tannadice are separated by just three hundred yards. They share the same street and are the closest two football stadiums in Britain. The modern view of the grounds is vastly different to the one which would have been observed in 1962. The 'multis', as the flats are known in Dundee, did not yet exist and the character of the grounds would have been altogether different, with traditional terracing and covered enclosures instead of the current box-work all-seater stands.

Dundee FC – formed in 1893 when two local clubs, East End and Our Boys, merged to gain entry into the Scottish League – moved into Dens Park in 1899. Their neighbours, then known as Dundee Hibernian, joined them next door ten years later. In its more than one hundred years of history, Dens Park has hosted two League Cup finals, League and Scottish Cup semi-finals, full internationals, a European Cup semi-final and a UEFA Fairs Cup semi-final.

On those occasions when supporters couldn't get into the ground for the big matches, there were some who would climb to the top of The Law to watch what they could through binoculars. The advent of live televised games has all but made this practice extinct. The last time that it was done to any large degree by Dundee fans was for the League Cup final against city rivals United at Dens in 1980. With the game not being transmitted live, hundreds of fans who couldn't get tickets climbed to the top of The Law armed with binoculars and radios. They must have yearned for the view of yesteryear, free from the intrusive 'multis' which now obscured the view of the goal at the TC Keay end.

Road transport in the early 1960s was still on the whole poor. To travel to any of the other Scottish city could take the best part of a day. There were few by-passes and no motorways, but the new road bridge would mark a dramatic improvement in road communications.

For the keener Dundee football fan, travel to away games was on the whole undertaken by train. But with two clubs in the city, football fans of either persuasion would often watch Dundee one week and United the other. United were for years the poorer relations, languishing in the Second Division. As such, they often earned sympathetic support from Dundee fans on matchdays when Dundee were playing away from home. This began to change in the 1960s, when United established themselves as a top division side and, indeed, finished above the Dark Blues in the league. This first happened in 1960-61, the season before Dundee were crowned champions.

Within the city, tramcars had been the main mode of transport, but the 1960s were to herald massive redevelopment in the town centre – not just to make way for the new Tay Road Bridge. Much of the character of the city centre was changed with the building of new 'modern' shopping malls. The first of these was the Overgate, which opened in 1964. Work on the Overgate was under way by the time Dundee won the championship, as the curious array of streets in and around the old Overgate Street made way for the new two-tier structure. They also made way for the Angus Hotel, which hosted Dundee FC's official centenary celebrations in 1993, attended by the 1962 league winning squad.

The trend was set, with the building of the Wellgate and Nethergate centres in later years, but when the League flag came to Dens Park the old Wellgate Street still ran up from the end of Murraygate to the bottom of the Hilltown. That would take you towards Dens, provided you could negotiate the steep climb.

Perhaps the most dramatic change to Dundee's landscape in the 1960s occurred on the north side of The Law. New estates were built to house the populace away from the outdated Victorian buildings in which many still lived. The estates of Fintry, Ardler, Menzieshill and Whitfield were 1960s creations, but the 'avenues of hope' in many places never lived up to expectations. Change was so rapid that the sight of men and woman sitting and singing in the back greens of the tenements was rapidly becoming a thing of the past.

Attendances at both Dundee football grounds fell in the 1960s, and despite the success that Dundee were briefly to enjoy, the trend was never properly bucked in the long term. The new housing estates that moved people to the periphery of the city was among the reasons blamed for this fall. Too many one-time supporters now lived in areas from which it was more difficult to travel to Dens or Tannadice.

Indeed, when Dundee went sixteen games unbeaten and led the First Division by six points around Christmas 1961, manager Bob Shankly made a public appeal for fans to come and support the team, as he insisted that the city had a team worth watching. He had a point. In two home games in December, Dens Park drew just 11,500 for games against Airdrie and Stirling Albion.

It was an appeal that succeeded to some extent towards the end of the season. Home crowds almost doubled in the run in, but the feeling was that the movement of the population towards the north of the city was having a permanently detrimental effect on crowds, no matter how good the results or performances were.

Lochee and its rich character had not yet been defaced by the roadways and concrete blocks which would destroy it many years later. In 1961-62 its maze of old streets and lanes still existed. Lochee had often been considered by Dundonians as almost a separate town – until the expansion of the conurbation – and had always been a rich vein of support for Dundee. Whenever the team toured the city after any trophy success, Lochee was certain to be on the route that the official party took. It still maintains its strong support for the club, with the Dee Club based in the area still following Dundee to home and away games.

Dundee was built on jute and the city became internationally known for its 'Three Js' – Jute, Jam and Journalism. By the beginning of the twentieth century there were 30,000 working in Dundee's jute mills in a population of 150,000. Jute gave Dundee its unique character. The smell of jute was in the air, in the same way that the smell from the breweries hung around the air in Edinburgh. The whiff of jute won't be easily forgotten by anyone who was brought up in Dundee in the first half of the twentieth century.

Jute contributed to every aspect of life in Dundee, not least its dialect, and it made the mill-owners rich. Many built themselves mansions in either Broughty Ferry or in the west end, near the Perth Road. Over the years many of the jute barons invested their money in shares in Dundee FC, and became directors on the board. This helped Dundee harbour a superior attitude over their poorer neighbours, Dundee United. United had originally been founded as Dundee Hibernian to cater for the poorer Irish immigrants of the city, although the support of Dundee has never in its history purported to be of a different social class to that of their rivals.

Jute, however, was in decline by the start of the 1960s, under threat from cheaper fabric abroad, and many of the bigger mills were beginning to close. Directly or indirectly, jute was still the biggest employer in the city, but the factory lifestyle was becoming harder to sustain, with long hours, filthy, noisy conditions for little money harping back to Victorian Britain. Today, little or no jute is made in Dundee and many of the great mills have been converted into private houses, flats or student accommodation around the city.

Jam and marmalade production at Keillors was another staple of Dundee life, as was the publishing firm DC Thomson, which produced titles such as the *Courier*, the *Sunday Post*, the *Dandy* and the *Beano*.

The corner of the now-vanished DM Browns on Commercial Street was a favourite meeting place for Dundonians and legend has it that Billy Steel was once found sitting on the pavement there by frantic Dundee staff, still drunk from the night before on the morning of a game. The story goes that he was taken up to Dens, given copious amounts of coffee and a cold shower, and he went out to score two goals.

There was far less consumer spending in those days, when the average working man earned around £400 a year. Luxuries were rare and even holidays for Dundonians were rarely taken further afield than Broughty Ferry. Fashions for the young were virtually non-existent. There were no discos or nightclubs; instead teenagers frequented coffee bars or cafes. One such coffee house, The Haparanda, of The Hap as it was known, in Arbroath Road, was popular with those who went to the football and it was often a meeting place for young fans before they headed up to Dens.

Like any Scottish city, Dundee had its share of pubs, most of which shut at 10pm and stayed shut on Sundays. There were thirteen picture houses, or cinemas, in the city in 1960. The choice wasn't so great for restaurants, however, with the main ones being Val D'Or, Keillors, Franchis and Kidds.

Football was by far the biggest sporting attraction in Dundee in the early 1960s, but during the summers cricket at Forthill in Broughty Ferry sometimes drew crowds as large as 1,000, especially when local rivals Perthshire played.

Boxing became popular in the city, thanks largely to the exploits of 21-year-old Dundonian Dick McTaggart, who won the lightweight gold medal at the 1956 Melbourne Olympic Games. Two thousand turned out to welcome him back to the city and he showed off his medal at Dundee's home against Rangers before a crowd of 28,500.

It was into this rapidly changing environment that Bob Shankly arrived in 1959. Redevelopment of Dens Park was well under way, having been initiated under previous boss Willie Thornton.

Thornton had replaced George Anderson in the summer of 1954. The former Rangers and Scotland centre-forward arrived at Dens when the good times appeared to be coming to an end. Already Cowan, Frew and Ziesing had left, Billy Steel's departure to America was imminent, Jimmy Toner had been given a free transfer, and Ronnie Turnbull was put up for sale. A number of the squad were also in the twilight of their careers and it was apparent to Thornton that a major rebuilding task had to be undertaken.

Thornton had been a somewhat surprising choice to succeed Anderson, as many had expected that trainer Reggie Smith would be offered the position. Back in 1949 Smith had been offered the job on a joint basis with Bobby Ancell, but had turned it down. Now, having gained coaching certificates both north and south of the border, he seemed the obvious candidate to succeed Anderson.

Smith was far from happy and in September he would set an example that was to be followed by Jim McLean in similar circumstances seventeen years later when he took the short walk down Tannadice Street to become manager of Dundee United.

To replace Smith, Thornton brought in former Arsenal player Archie MacAuley as his right-hand man. MacAuley had played in the same Great Britain side as Billy Steel against the Rest of Europe in 1949 but his ideas of coaching and tactics were radically different to those that had been used under 'Toffee Dod'. Instead of an open attacking style, MacAuley wanted Dundee to defend deep, retreating to their eighteen-yard line, when the opposition had the ball. These tactics became unpopular with established players such as internationalist Doug Cowie. MacAuley insisted that his ways were right, reasoning that Dundee weren't good enough to play the attacking football for which he had been renowned in his playing career.

Thornton had been keen to model his side on Rangers' defensive style of the time and although it had served the Ibrox side well, the results at Dens just did not come. Thornton didn't want the forward line to go more than three men up, and by mid-March 1955 Dundee hovered ominously near the relegation zone.

Thornton, however, had been willing to give youth its chance. Despite the poor results, youngsters such as George O'Hara and Alan Cousin had impressed, and it was hoped that other new signings, like Bobby Cox from local side Osbourne and George McGeachie from Falkirk High, would do likewise. Cox and McGeachie would become members of the Dundee side that would win the championship several years later, as would Alan Cousin who was the first of that side to make his breakthrough into the Dundee first team.

Cousin was signed from Alloa YMCA at the age of sixteen in 1955. By the time Dundee won the Scottish League championship he was the club's longest serving player at just 24 years of age. Cousin was delighted to get a chance in a side that included big names like Doug Cowie, Bill Brown and Danny Malloy, and as a tall, hard-hitting centre-forward, he was able to hold his own from an early age. He became known as the 'king of the double shuffle' and formed a potent partnership with Alan Gilzean. In total, Cousin made 362 appearances for Dundee, scoring 141 goals. An ever-present in the championship season, Cousin scored nineteen times and became the first British player to score in the San Siro when Dundee lost 1-5 to AC Milan in the first leg of the European Cup semi-final in 1963.

Football, however, did not become a full-time profession for Cousin, who remained part-time at Dens to attend St Andrews University. There he studied Greek and Latin for an Arts degree, becoming a secondary school language teacher in his home town of Alloa after completing a teacher training degree in Dundee. Whilst at university, Cousin trained on his own with a regime prepared by Archie McAuley on the St Andrews' beach – a beach later made famous in the introduction to 'Chariots of Fire'. When Cousin graduated to the classroom, he trained three nights a week with Falkirk. There was no fear, however, that all his brains had gone to his head for, during his time at Dens, Cousin gained international caps for the Scottish League, and at Under-23 and youth level.

Cousin made his Dundee league debut on 3 March 1956, in a 1-3 defeat at Falkirk. His first goal in a Dark Blue shirt came in a friendly at Dens Park in April, when new English champions Manchester United came to town and were whipped 5-1. It was a result which lifted Dundee's spirits to the extent that they won three of their last four games to stave off the threat of relegation. Nevertheless, Dundee's final position of thirteenth, albeit in an expanded eighteen-club division, was their lowest since gaining promotion in 1947. The team was evidently going backwards, which must have saddened George Anderson, who passed away aged 69.

During the summer of 1956 Thornton rejected an offer to manage Preston North End, preferring to concentrate on building his youth policy at Dens, but the pressure was now on him to produce results. In the short term they did, for Dundee reached the semi-final of the League Cup, losing to Partick Thistle 2-3 in an Ibrox replay. In the previous round Dundee had knocked out Dundee United in a two-legged affair, the first leg of which has been immortalised in song. United were still in Division Two at that time, and crashed 3-7 – Dundee's Jimmy Chalmers scoring four. Dark Blue fans commemorated the result by reworking the words of the traditional Scottish song, 'We're no awa tae bide awa'.'

As I was walking doon the Overgate, / I met wee Johnnie Scobie,
And he said to me, / Would you like to see,
The Famous Dundee FC / So I went along to Dens Park,
To see the famous eleven, / And when we got there,
The terracing was bare, / But we gave United seven!'

That song is still sung at Dens today, and was reworked a second time for a more modern version, released as part of the 'It's My Dundee' CD by the JMB Dundee Supporters Club in 2000. The new version, entitled 'The New Johnnie Scobie' retained the references to 'giving United seven' and was adopted by the club as its official anthem for 2000-01. It was played every time the team ran out onto the park that season.

The fact that United won the second leg 2-1 at Tannadice counted for nothing. Dundee were through to the semis and the damage to United's reputation had been done.

Within a week of losing that semi-final, Thornton gave a debut to the player who would skipper the Dark Blues to their title triumph. Bobby Cox, known as 'Sir Robert' to the Dundee support today, made a keen start to his 327 league appearances in a 3-1 home win over Queens Park. The 22-year-old went on to make 30 appearances at right-back that season and soon became a favourite with the fans. He became known for his trademark sliding tackle with the outside of his right foot, and after he retired he opened a pub in Broughty Ferry named The Sliding Tackle.

Around the time that Cox was making his breakthrough, Billy Steel, now 33, wrote to Thornton asking if he could return to Dens Park for a trial. Things had not gone well for Steel in America. He had signed for the Los Angeles Danes, but after six games was dropped. He incurred further wrath from his new club when he was accused of a traffic violation. He moved to San Francisco, where he didn't kick a ball in eighteen months and, after seemingly kickstarting his career at Hollywood FC in January 1956, he thought he would try his luck with Dundee, claiming that he still had a couple of season left in him.

In typical Steel style, however, nothing more was heard from him, even though Thornton had written back agreeing to his request. The manager refocused of his youth policy and, by the end of that season, Bobby Cox, Alan Cousin, George McGeachie, George O'Hara, Davie Esson, Dave Sneddon, Jackie Stewart, Dougie Alexander, Jim Ferguson (a defender) and another Jim Ferguson (a goalkeeper) had all tasted first-team action. Dundee finished tenth.

Kilmarnock offered the Rugby Park hot seat to Thornton that summer, but with the arrival of Alan Gilzean from Coupar Angus Juniors, Alex Hamilton from Dundee North End, Hugh Robertson from Auchinleck Talbot, and Jimmy Gabriel from Dundee North End, it would have been a shortsighted manager who would have turned his back on the crop of talent at his disposal at Dens Park. Both Robertson and Hamilton made their debuts in season 1957-58, by the end of which Cox, Hamilton, Robertson and Cousin were established first-team regulars. In fact, Cox was the only ever present.

Cox's full-back partner, Alex Hamilton, had made his debut in August at Hearts in the League Cup, but had to wait until December for his first league start. Despite a 1-7 defeat at Airdrie, Hamilton kept his place for the rest of the season at the expense of the injured Hugh Reid.

Hugh Robertson had been given his chance in September at Pittodrie, and like Hammy a debut defeat did not harm the left winger's long-term chances. Hugh (or Shug as it is shortened to in Scots) went on to make 25 appearances in his debut year, pitching in with four goals.

Dundee finished 1957-58 a lowly eleventh, with just 31 points, half the total of champions Hearts, but the promise shown by the youngsters gave hope of a brighter future. Alan Cousin top-scored with 23 goals and was capped at Under-23 level against Holland. In the last game of the season, goalkeeper Pat Liney made his debut in a 1-0 win at Ibrox.

The void left by trainer Reggie Smith's departure to Tannadice had also been filled earlier that season. The man brought in to assist Willie Thornton would become a key figure in Dundee's league winning success, and also become Bob Shankly's right-hand man – Sammy Kean.

Kean had been a one-man club until his appointment at Dens as trainer-coach in 1957. He had spent his entire senior career at Hibs, joining the club in 1947 from junior club Kirkintilloch Rob Roy. He had played for the Easter Road club at wing-half for nine years before stepping through the grades of assistant trainer and then trainer in the year before he came to Dundee.

Kean had won a league championship medal during his time with Hibs and had played in the same team as the Hibs 'Famous Five' forward line, which included Gordon Smith. Kean would be instrumental in persuading 'the Gay Gordon' to join Dundee in 1961. Kean had attempted to persuade Smith to come two years earlier, on the player's release from Hibs, but finally got the man many considered to be the final piece in the Dundee championship jigsaw.

Much of the credit for the players' improved fitness levels is down to Kean. Dundee's most capped player, Alex Hamilton, later described him as the 'perfect back-up man for Shankly as they put their ideas together'. Kean was also partly responsible for the signing of Ian Ure, one of the greatest players ever to wear the dark blue of Dundee and Scotland.

Ure arrived at Dens as a trialist in 1958. He spent a week attempting to impress Willie Thornton, after which the Dundee boss shook his head and prepared to allow the youngster to return home to Ayr. Sammy Kean persuaded Thornton to keep Ure on for another week, but the manager was no more impressed by the blond defender after two weeks than after one. Kean again stepped in, told Thornton that his judgment was questionable, and insisted that he sign the 6ft 1in defender. Mercifully, Kean's assessment prevailed.

Ure was offered £100 to sign and the man described by BBC commentator Kenneth Wolstenholme before Scotland's 2-1 Wembley win over England in 1963 as 'the greatest centre-half in the world today' went on to make 133 league appearances for Dundee before moving to Arsenal later that year. Thornton, however, was never totally won over. Despite giving Ure his debut in December 1958 in a home win over Falkirk, the player had to wait until the arrival of Bob Shankly before he established himself.

Season 1958-59 began with wins over Aberdeen and Rangers at Ibrox, whereupon the *Daily Record* correspondent described Dundee as a side who 'have the makings of a team who could win the Scottish Cup'. How wrong he was. Dundee crashed out in the first round to Highland League side Fraserburgh – one of the biggest shocks in Scottish football history. The fact that it was a last-minute goal by Fraserburgh that did the damage hardly eased the humiliation. Alan Cousin describes the defeat as the main memory from his early years at Dens. For Cowie and Brown, it was particularly painful, for they had both played in the Berwick debacle in 1954.

Away from the Scottish Cup, things seemed to be progressing nicely. Cox, Hamilton and Gabriel were now well established in the Dundee defence. Alongside them was the veteran Doug Cowie who, along with goalkeeper Bill Brown, had represented Scotland at the World Cup finals in Sweden the previous summer.

In February 1959, a month after the Fraserburgh shock, Thornton handed a debut to the youngest player ever to play for Dundee. Andy Penman had only just arrived at Dens Park, having returned homesick from Everton. Despite being just short of his sixteenth birthday, the Fife lad debuted in a 3-0 home win against Third Lanark. With hindsight, the Cup exit served to strengthen the team, which embarked on a nine-game unbeaten run which lifted them to fourth, their highest placing in eight years.

Some of Dundee's younger starlets were already attracting attention. Alan Cousin had already been the subject of a £16,500 bid from Rangers but, as he was studying at St Andrew's University, Cousin was happy enough to remain at Dens. Dundee were not so lucky when Tottenham Hotspur came knocking on the door for Bill Brown. The goalkeeper's fee, curiously, was also £16,500, the same as that offered for Cousin. Brown would do well for Spurs, cementing his reputation as one of the best goalkeepers in Britain.

Brown was not the only big name to leave Dens Park that summer. One month into the 1959-60 season, manager Willie Thornton resigned and returned to Glasgow on account of his wife's ill health. He had only recently turned down an offer to manage relegated Leeds United, but his personal circumstances now forced him to uproot from the east coast and take up the job of managing Partick Thistle.

Thornton had not found it easy in his first managerial role, losing so many stars from George Anderson's successful side, and his time at Dens Park was essentially a period of transition, signing young players and trying to rebuild the side.

The development of the 'Thornton Babes' must have made the Dens Park job an attractive one in the 'vacant positions' column. Just before he departed, Thornton had given young Alan Gilzean his debut at home to

Motherwell in a 1-4 League Cup defeat. After the game Gilzean had to dash back to Aldershot where he was completing his National Service. Bobby Waddell, who played five times in the championship season, was given his debut by Thornton the week after 'Gillie'.

In short, there was an abundance of young talent at Dens to entice an ambitious man. The man in question turned out to be 48-year-old Bob Shankly, whose first managerial appointment had been at Falkirk, and who now gave up his job with Third Lanark to come to Dundee.

Shankly had been in senior football for 29 years, having emerged from the coalmining pits to sign for Alloa in 1930. Bob was one of five brothers who had all played for a little Ayrshire village side called the Glenbuck Cherry Pickers. It might easily have been another brother, Bill, who took charge at Dens. Bill Shankly, then manager of Huddersfield Town, would go on to make his name as the architect of the modern Liverpool Football Club. But he might not have done so. He made a late application for the vacant Dundee position on the very day that his brother Bob was appointed. But Bob, with his quiet, unassuming efficiency made Dundee into an outstanding team which his brother would have struggled to match. It is nevertheless an intriguing question. What might Bill have done at Dens, given what he was about to do at Anfield?

Bob had been transferred to Falkirk for a fee of £100 three years after joining Alloa and played for the Bairns for fifteen years before coaching neighbours Stenhousemuir. He returned to Brockville in time to sit in the home dug-out when Dundee lost the championship of the last day of 1948-49, and there is little doubt that observing Dundee's collapse that day that would stand in him in good stead in his own title chase in the spring of 1962.

In seven years at Falkirk, Shankly showed himself to be shrewd in the transfer market. He sold players to the value of £80,000 without damaging the playing side, and when at the Hi-His he halved the Cathkin debt of £18,000. In his two years at Thirds, Shankly built a Scottish Cup semi-final side out of nothing. Before quitting to join Dundee in October 1959, he had already guided Third Lanark to the League Cup final, which they lost 1-2 to Hearts in the wake of his departure.

Shankly relished the challenge ahead of him and the prospect of building on the youth policy which Thornton had established. There was much work to be done, however, as Dundee had started 1959-60 badly, having won only three out of thirteen matches when he joined. His baptism saw Dundee go down 1-3 at home to Rangers.

Shankly's line up that afternoon was: Liney, Hamilton, Cox, Gabriel, Smith, Curlett, McGeachie, Cousin, Hill, Henderson and Robertson. Of those eleven, six would pick up championship medals in 1962. Despite the promise at Dens, therefore, there was plenty to be done, but with youngsters such as Gilzean, Ure and Penman already at the club, the fundamentals were in place.

By Christmas, young Penman had become at automatic choice for the No 7 shirt. Gilzean, the last Dundee player to perform National Service, returned to Dundee in February for a 0-0 draw at Ibrox. Gillie did well enough to retain his place the following week at home to St Mirren. It turned out to be a historic day as Gilzean scored his first goal for the club and his first goal in senior football. His well-placed header was Dundee's opening goal in a 3-1 win. Gilzean would become renowned for his aerial power and heading ability, first with Dundee, then for Scotland and Tottenham, and so it was perhaps no surprise that the first of his 165 goals in his seven years with Dundee came with his head.

Financially, Dundee were on a sound financial footing when Shankly arrived, thanks largely to the sale of Bill Brown, but despite assurances from the board that Dundee's young talent was not for sale, they found it impossible to resist Everton's offer of £30,000 for centre-half Jimmy Gabriel.

Shankly left the decision about staying or going to the player himself, and was reportedly upset when Gabriel opted to move south. His sale also provoked angry protests from Dundee fans, but they were quickly appeased when Ian Ure stepped into the breach.

The money from the sale of Brown and Gabriel funded the installations of floodlights at Dens and the construction of a covered enclosure opposite the main stand which could accommodate 10,000 spectators. The floodlights were officially switched on for an evening visit by Bill Shankly's Liverpool. The date was 23 March 1960, and the Dark Blues defeated Second Division Liverpool 1-0 through a Hugh Robertson goal which sailed in direct from a corner-kick past future Dees goalkeeper Bert Slater.

Gilzean had come off the bench as a substitute against Liverpool and done enough to earn a starting slot for most of the games remaining. In four starts, Gilzean scored six goals, including his first hat-trick. The victims were Stirling Albion. Unbeaten in their final seven games, the Dark Blues finished a credible fourth. Gilzean had arrived and so it appeared had Dundee.

Shankly realised, however, that his young guns needed some experienced heads. In August 1960 he pulled off something of a coup by signing Monifieth-born Bobby Seith, a right-half who had just captained Burnley to the English First Division championship. Seith was happy to return to his native Tayside and for £6,000 Shankly had got a bargain in the 29-year-old.

Alan Gilzean would soon be banging in goals for fun. In season 1960-61 he scored a total of 32 goals in all competitions. For a number of years Dundee had been a decent footballing side without a real killer touch, but Gilzean now provided it.

Ian Ure also established himself that season when he moved to centre-half to replace the injured Billy Smith. Ure had broken through to the first team as understudy to Doug Cowie in the No 6 jersey, but the injury to Smith saw Ure switch to centre-half, where he never looked back. He made 41 appearances that season in his new position.

Shankly, though, was still seeking greater experience and in December made Dundee's second attempt to sign Gordon Smith from Hearts. The need to bolster the squad was heightened by leg and ankle breaks for McGeachie and Penman respectively. In January 1961 Shankly bought left-half Bobby Wishart from Aberdeen for £3,500. Wishart make an immediate mark for the Dark Blues, scoring twice on his debut in a 3-0 home win over Dundee United, who were now in their first season back in Division One.

Much of that campaign, however, was hampered by injury, and Shankly was forced to experiment with players moving to new positions throughout the season. Gilzean, for example, was moved to inside-right and then inside-left, while Wishart moved to left-half in place of Cowie. Dundee finished that season down in tenth position, after some erratic results and performances.

Even worse, Dundee United had finished above Dundee for the first time in their history –- one place and one point better off. But Shankly believed that his troops were on the right path. Rangers were still at that time the team to beat. They had won eight league championships since the War, but Hearts, Hibs and Aberdeen had also got their hands on the championship trophy to show that it was possible for a provincial club to win the league.

Scottish football had changed dramatically since 1945 and was enjoying its most competitive era when many clubs could realistically chase success. Never before or since had the the Old Firm been so vulnerable. Clyde, Motherwell, Hearts, Hibs, Falkirk, St Mirren, Dunfermline, Aberdeen, East Fife, and of course Dundee, had all won major trophies since the War. Bob Shankly's Dundee were ready to charge to the top.

Chapter 3

~ Confidence and Belief ~

(July – November 1961)

Over the years, there had been a succession of bonnie Dundee teams but by 1961, the bonnets of Dundee had seldom been tossed into the air to salute success. On only three occasions had Juteopolis enjoyed revelry in the wee sma' hours to celebrate the winning of a major honour, and that was hardly good enough for a club with Dundee's resources. Dundee had often produced great players and couldn't complain about a lack of support, actual and potential, so it was a mystery as to why Dundee had never quite lived up to their potential in almost 70 years of existence. In the summer of 1961, in the annual *Scottish Football Book*, Hugh Taylor attempted an explanation and cited two reasons:

Firstly, 'Dundee have always been noted for entertainment, playing with a refreshing zest, gaiety and colour with unorthodox touches, but they have often lacked the killer touch. Dundee have always been known as the "Dapper Dans" of Scottish football as they have been fascinating to watch but without a real goal lust or the devastating finishing of real champions. Dundee were often advocates of "good form" and went for technique in a big way and often it appeared that style was of more importance to Dundee than winning.'

Secondly, Taylor suggested that Dundee had been guilty in the past of transferring too many of their stars. In recent years, 'their supporters have had cause for complaint when the likes of Jimmy Gabriel, Danny Malloy and Bill Brown have all gone south to English clubs to boost Dundee's bank balance by £70,000.'

By 1961, however, both of these factors had seemingly changed. There had been signs the previous season that, despite the disappointing league position, that Dundee had adopted a 'new policy'.

The Dark Blues appeared to have already solved their ancient problem of finding an attack with goalscoring punch. Young Alan Gilzean's aerial power and whiplash shooting had already bagged 42 goals in 50 appearances for the club. Added to this, Alan Cousin had pitched in with an average rate of nineteen goals per season in the last four years. All in all, Dundee's attack now looked more potent than at any other stage in her history.

Dundee also appeared to have stemmed the flow of talent that had always haemorrhaged out of the club. Despite a number of English clubs buzzing around Dens in the last twelve months, none of Dundee's rising stars had been lured away. Bob Shankly publicly stated that none of his talent was for sale, hinting that he was in the process of building something special. He told the *Daily Record* in May 1961: 'I am in the process of building a team here and none of my squad will be leaving. I am confident we are close to taking the next step and creating some special times at Dens.' (Craig Brown, in his autobiography, tells how Shankly, like his brother Bill at Liverpool, liked to talk up in his players and his club in the press at every opportunity.)

Hugh Taylor seemingly agreed. In the *Scottish Football Book* he wrote: 'If Dundee are as good as their word and hold onto their splendid new young players, they could soon be at the summit of the football world.' Taylor himself put the mid-table finish in the previous campaign down to an 'unfortunate crop of injuries' and one hopes that he backed his predictions with the bookmakers, because Dundee started their championship campaign as 20-1 outsiders for the league title.

The youth policy begun by Willie Thornton was beginning to bear fruit. During the former Ibrox idol's five years in the Dens Park hot seat, he had signed no fewer than 72 players. Shankly now took up the baton, looking to add more experienced faces to the squad.

Shankly was a down-to-earth character, described by Alan Gilzean as 'an honest man who would call a spade a spade'. He was a real 'working manager'. For Shankly there was no public flamboyancy, no red carnation or the rich cigar, and he wasn't one of those football bosses who just talked a good game. He would rather get his jacket off and get down to the gruelling business of football with his players. If there was one man who could rid Dundee of the 'Dainty Dinah' or 'Dapper Dans' tags, it was Bob Shankly.

One thing that did concern Shankly was the supply line to his big forwards. For the third time, Dundee sought the services of Gordon Smith (described as the 'Stanley Matthews of Scottish Football' by Jim Wilkie in *Across the Great Divide: A History of Professional Football In Dundee.*) Trainer Sammy Kean, a former team-mate of Smith's, helped persuade him to join Dundee. But at 37, many fans wondered how much mileage was in Smith's legs, particularly as Hearts had given him a free transfer.

There was no arguing over Smith's pedigree. He had four championship medals from Hibs (three) and Hearts (one) and had captained his country. Smith's signature in the summer of 1961 was a master-stroke which would complete the jigsaw of Dundee's championship side.

Raised in Montrose, Smith had played for Dundee junior side Dundee North End before signing for Hibs in 1941 for a £10 signing on fee. The most graceful of outside-rights, Smith played at Easter Road for eighteen years, during which time he collected three league championship medals and reached a European Cup semi-final. He earned 30 international caps, two as captain, and was Scottish Player of the Year in 1951.

The press dubbed him the 'Gay Gordon' (after the Scottish country dance) or the 'Gay Cavalier', whose meanings today would carry different connotations. Smith was described in the Dundee v Cologne European Cup match programme in September 1962 as 'the greatest Soccer pin up north of the border since the War'. An athletic, 5ft 9in tall figure, with short, dark, wavy hair in a middle parting, Smith's attractive style was matched both on and off the field.

John Cairney, who would list Smith among the top 100 players in his *Scottish Football Hall of Fame*, says: 'His grace on the run, cloaking a deceptive speed, allowed him to seize on half-chances around the goal area, hence his high tally of goals. Beneath the superficial attraction, was true football steel, as his three hundred goals showed and as his three Scottish Championship medals with three different clubs amply demonstrates.'

Smith had been freed by Hibs in 1959, when a queue of clubs, including Dundee, chased his signature. He chose to stay in Edinburgh, spending two years with Hearts, with whom he won another title in 1960.

At Hearts, no longer so swift of foot, Smith fell back into the role of playmaker, according to John Cairney, 'the architect rather than the builder'. His unique achievement of winning championship medals with three different clubs, none of which was Rangers or Celtic, is described by historian Bob Crampsey as 'the greatest individual accomplishment in the entire history of Scottish League Football'. In view of his age, Smith's achievements at Dens are extraordinary. In total he played 89 games in three seasons, scoring nineteen times. In the championship season he played 37 games and bettered that a year later with 48.

There have been few more graceful players in Scottish football than Gordon Smith and it was his exemplary attention to fitness that ensured that he could endure at the top level for 23 years. He also paid attention to his diet and was keen to hear about the eating habits of footballers on the continent. He would, for example, introduce his team-mates to such things as pasta long before it was a popular footballers' dish.

Having played football in Edinburgh for twenty years, Smith had a grocer's business in the capital and lived in North Berwick, to the south of city. He decided to stay there and commute to Dens by motor car. The journey would mean a 5.30am daily rise.

Smith joined his new team-mates for pre-season training on 28 June. They faced a week of intensive training before heading to Iceland for an eight-day, three-game pre-season tour.

Before they departed, a row broke out between the club and Doug Cowie, who had been given a free transfer after sixteen years at Dens. Cowie had won two League Cups, played in two World Cup finals, and earned twenty international caps. His departure severed the last connection with George Anderson's golden years. While, at 34, Cowie felt he still had a couple of years left, it appeared to many that Shankly had purposefully rid the club of the last of the Anderson old boys. Cowie felt even more aggrieved by the arrival of Gordon Smith, who was three years his senior, but in July he joined Morton as player-coach, on the apparent understanding that he could still train at Dens.

Shankly, however, balked at the idea of letting any non-Dundee player train with his first team. He issued an instruction that only DFC players would be welcome at Dens in the mornings, although guests would be permitted to train at the ground in the afternoons and evenings.

Cowie went public, claiming that he had been banned from Dens altogether. Shankly denied this but Cowie was aggrieved at being barred from access to Dens even after hours. 'The office staff need time off as well and need to go home too,' replied Shankly, expressing disappointment that Cowie should publicly run his old club down.

'I don't think I suited Shankly's style,' Doug Cowie now says diplomatically of his acrimonious departure. 'As the last of George Anderson's favourites, I think he was maybe looking for a clean sweep.' Cowie instead turned to Jerry Kerr at Dundee United for training facilities, and returned years later as a scout for Jim McLean at Tannadice, where he helped recruit much young local talent in his 23 years there.

Minus Cowie, Dundee flew out to Iceland on 4 July. Craig Brown describes his excitement at visiting 'a country that I had only read about and been fascinated by, never considering that I would actually be seeing it one day.' The flight carrying the twenty-strong party from Renfrew to Reykjavik was delayed for four hours by seagulls fouling an engine. The club stayed at the Hotel Garden in Reykjavik and were determined to forge links while in Europe's northernmost capital. Club secretary Bob Crighton carried goodwill letters from Dundee Lord Provost, Maurice McManus, to hand to the Icelandic civic authorities.

The first match was against KR Reykjavik, where Gordon Smith made his debut in a Dundee shirt by notching the first goal in a 3-1 win. Andy Penman and Bobby Waddell scored the others for an under-strength side minus Bobby Cox and Alan Gilzean, who had both undergone minor knee surgery. Both, however, played in the next game, on 12 July, against Icelandic champions Akranes, with eight Icelandic internationalists. The Dees won 4-0 and the local press described Dundee as, apart from Moscow Dynamo, 'the best side ever to play in Iceland.' The goals came from Cousin, Penman (2), and Smith, whose second goal in two games excited the Dundee press, in the shape of ex-player Tommy Gallacher. (Gallacher, a member of Anderson's '50s side, wrote for the Dundee *Courier* for 29 years and was a well-loved and well-respected journalist on both sides of Dundee's footballing divide.)

Young Craig Brown impressed, playing the full 90 minutes at left-half. Brown had been Bob Shankly's first signing for Dundee, arriving on loan from Rangers in January 1960. The move was made permanent that summer when Dundee agreed a £8,000 fee. Brown – who would go on to be Scotland's longest serving international manager – was also, curiously, the last player Shankly sold, when he joined Falkirk in 1965, shortly before Shankly himself departed. In between times, the 5ft 7in fair-haired, crew-cutted Brown would make just fifteen appearances for Dundee over five years, but his career was severely hampered by the knee injury which eventually forced his retirement. Brown always travelled with the first-team squad, but with no substitutes at that time his appearances were limited. He, himself, says that if substitutes had been introduced earlier he would have made a record number of appearances from the bench.

Brown remembers his time at Dens with fondness. When asked, for example, why he picked Gavin Rae for his Scottish squad against Poland in April 2001 (Rae became the first Dundee player to represent Scotland in fifteen years), Brown replied, 'because he plays for Dundee'.

When Brown became Scotland manager in 1993, the Scottish press asked 'Craig who?' When challenged to show his medals, he silenced the west coast journalists by saying he had a Dundee championship medal, to which his nine games in 1961-62 entitled him.

Dundee finished their schedule on 12 July against an Iceland international select. Gilzean and Hugh Robertson (2) scored in a 3-1 win, which meant that Dundee would fly home with a 100 per cent record.

That game is remembered for the referee pushing Bobby Cox – who had queried a decision – in the chest, then sending him off. Afterwards it transpired that the official had not sent Cox off, even thought the player left the field, but had only issued a reprimand. The dismissal would not therefore count against Cox on his disciplinary record.

On the last evening, a dinner dance was held by the tour's sponsors, Throltor FC, and the Dundee players were each given a sheepskin rug. The directors were presented with a 'replica of a falcon'.

Shankly gave his players a week off before reassembling on 20 July. Five of the squad took part in a five-a-side competition at Gayfield Park, contested by Dundee, Dundee United, Montrose, Brechin City, St Johnstone and hosts Arbroath. Dundee's 'fivesome' were Bobby Cox, Alex Hamilton, Hugh Reid, Bobby Seith and Alan Gilzean, each taking turns to go in goal. There was no trainer or physio with them, otherwise Gilzean might have been whisked back home after the knee which had recently undergone surgery puffed up. Dundee beat Montrose, lost to Dundee United, then beat Arbroath in the final.

Gilzean missed a few days' training, as did Alan Cousin, a full-time teacher. Cousin would follow his own pre-season routine, while George McGeachie was also set to go part-time when he started teacher training in August. Another part-time player, Bobby Wishart, had a job with an insurance firm. Wishart passed his driving test in July to help him in his full-time profession.

On 1 August Shankly gave his players a rest day, which they spent playing golf or football on the beach at Monifieth. Team-spirit was good. Several players lodged together in club digs. Ian Ure, Hugh Robertson, Craig Brown, Tommy Mackle, George Ryden and Alan Gilzean – when he didn't go home to Coupar Angus – all shared digs in the city, and Craig Brown tells about the practical jokes played on each other. For example, they made a habit of buying the Dundee *Evening Telegraph* before Ian Ure and spoiling his fun by doing the crossword before him. Big Ian liked to throw down a challenge to see who could finish it first, and it took him weeks to realise that the reason he was always last was because the rest had done it at lunchtime.

Ure, Robertson, Ryden, Brown and Mackle became known as the 'Garvie Five' as their landlady was a Mrs Garvie. They were notoriously late for training as the car they shared had a habit of refusing to start.

Brown describes the Dundee squad as an intelligent bunch. Brown himself was a secondary school teacher in Dundee, while Alan Cousin was teaching in Alloa. When Georgie McGeachie started teacher training in 1961, Dundee had their fair share of bookish qualifications. Gilzean, too, speaks highly of his team-mates on and off the park. They were growing together, both as players and as people. Bobby Cox endorses the idea of a fine group of people coming together at the right time.

On 7 August, five days before the start of the new season, Dundee held their annual public trial, in which the entire playing staff competed in a full-scale practice match. The match consisted of three periods of 30 minutes, normal for trial matches. The Dundee first team played in white against the reserves in blue. It was the first chance for the 5,500 crowd to see Gordon Smith in a Dundee shirt at Dens, but the Gay Gordon only played fifteen minutes, hampered by a toe injury sustained in Iceland. In total, 31 players took the field and the Whites won 5-2.

The Whites called upon two goalkeepers, Pat Liney and 17-year-old Ally Donaldson – who would have to wait three years for his first-team debut. For the moment, Shankly felt that Donaldson was too raw to be in contention for a first-team place, and toyed with signing Arbroath's Leslie Cameron and Butterburn Youth keeper Sandy Davie. As a result, Shankly was on the lookout for a back-up keeper throughout the championship season.

The build up to the first game saw just light training on Thursday and Friday. The main injury worry concerned Gordon Smith's toe. Dundee's season began on the 'Glorious Twelfth' (the start of the Grouse-shooting season) with a home League Cup-tie against Airdrie.

The League Cup had been the traditional season-opener almost since its inception. The first stage took the form of four-team sections, played home and away, the winners progressing to the knock-out phase. Dundee's section was tough, comprising three other Division One sides – Third Lanark, Airdrie, and champions and League Cup holders Rangers. Dundee had just done the league double over the Gers, so relished the challenge ahead of them.

Scottish football had a buoyancy about it at that time. Real Madrid's fabulous 7-3 European Cup win over Eintracht Frankfurt at Hampden a year earlier had whetted appetites. Ian Ure was one of many who drooled in wonder at the magic shown by Real's Puskas and Co. Ure promised himself to work harder at his game, often staying behind after training to practise his ball control. In fact, just before the season started he set a new personal record of 2,880 keepie-uppies!

Shankly's team showed only one change in personnel from that which had kicked off the 1960-61 campaign – Bobby Wishart in for Billy Smith. Gordon Smith's toe kept him out and there were some positional changes from the side that had opened against Raith twelve months previously. Ian Ure, who had then played at left-half, was now centre-half instead of the injured Billy Smith. Wishart filled Ure's No 6 shirt. Andy Penman continued in the inside-right slot which he had tried in Iceland. With Doug Cowie now departed, Bobby Cox led Dundee out for the first time as the club's captain.

Dundee's glory season got off to a flyer when Wishart struck from the edge of the box after just three minutes. Admission to the terracing was three shillings (15p) but the 13,000 crowd had to wait until the second half for the clinching goal when Cousin netted from close range.

The 2-0 win could not disguise the poverty of the performance and Shankly sighed: 'The boys just had one of those days.'

It was Rangers next at Ibrox, a ground where Dundee had not lost a league game since 1957. Gordon Smith had to face criticism from the press and fans that he seemed to be picking and choosing his matches. Smith pointed out that he had a broken toe, so could hardly play against Airdrie or Rangers even if he wanted to.

Smith wasn't the only casualty. Gilzean also missed the Ibrox game when he failed a fitness test on his suspect knee. Bobby Waddell took his place. Waddell had scored six goals in twelve games the previous year and had scored against Rangers two years before, so was capable of inflicting damage of his own.

However, Rangers' Ralph Brand scored twice in a minute before a 40,000 Ibrox crowd, the biggest to watch Dundee all season. Penman and Cousin levelled by the interval, but the second half didn't quite go to plan. While never a dirty game, the tackling was hard and Bobby Seith was booked for a foul on Davie Wilson. Unlike today, bookings were rare in earlier times, and throughout the whole of the 1961-62 season Dundee picked up just three cautions and had no one sent off. Wilson restored Rangers' lead in the 71st minute and Jimmy Millar made sure the two League Cup points stayed in Govan when he headed home a Wilson free-kick to give Rangers a 4-2 victory.

Filling in for Gordon Smith at Ibrox was George McGeachie, whom Alan Gilzean rated as a player despite his often seeming more interested in his career off the pitch. Gilzean felt McGeachie was unlucky to lose his place after the signing of Gordon Smith. George had played seventeen times the previous campaign and in total would make 100 appearances for the Dark Blues. He had debuted in 1957 but would make just five appearances in the title season. He left the club in December 1963 to sign for Darlington and work for ICI on Teesside.

Dundee's hopes of qualifying from their group were all but dashed by a 2-3 defeat at Third Lanark. That left Shankly's men four points behind Rangers, who had won their first three games. But the loss to the Hi-His (a sort-of acronym of Third Lanark) did contain some plusses for the Dees. Gordon Smith made his competitive debut and marked the occasion with his first goal for the club, but overall 'The Gay Cavalier' had a quiet match and for long spells looked almost lost. He lacked understanding with his inside-right, Penman, who was himself new to his position. Also, Gilzean returned after injury and opened his account for the season when he headed in a Hugh Robertson cross. Gilzean had scored thirteen goals in the previous season's League Cup, when Dundee had topped their section, but barring some extraordinary results in the matches to come, he was unlikely to get close to that figure. Nevertheless, 40 goals in 50 Dundee games meant that Gilzean was indisputably the team's main goal threat.

With the League Cup section half-completed, Dundee now opened their league campaign with a Wednesday trip to Falkirk, scene of their biggest heartache, back in 1949. When Hearts lost the championship to Celtic on the last day of 1985-86 in similar circumstances – losing at Dens when they needed only to draw – older Dundee supporters could empathise. Among them was my father, who had been at Brockville on that fateful day. Since 1986, whenever Dundee entertain Hearts, some home fans still chant the name of Albert Kidd, who came off the bench to sink Hearts with two late goals, but they tend to be younger fans. They weren't old enough to have lived through Dundee's own last-day collapse. Nor should it be forgotten that in 1961-62 the Brockville nightmare was still fresh in the memory for many supporters.

For this latest trip to Brockville, Shankly kept faith with the eleven who had lost at Cathkin Park. They would soon become household names, for with few exceptions they would be first choices thereafter. Gordon Smith rediscovered his rhythm and dashed up the wing in his old accustomed style, scoring his first league goal for his new club. The *Courier* described Smith's display as 'back to his gayest'. In addition to his goal, he set up Dundee's two others with deft crosses that were planted in Falkirk's net by firm headers. Gilzean did not look fully fit, and Hugh Robertson picked up a knock in the second half to leave Dundee playing out time with ten men.

Falkirk's only reply was a Wyles shot through the gloaming in the dying seconds. With the game starting at 7.30pm on a Wednesday (23 August), Falkirk decided not to switch on their floodlights, reasoning that there would be plenty of natural light by the scheduled finish at 9.10. But by 9 darkness had descended upon Brockville, so that when Wyles scored Liney complained that he couldn't see the ball. No mention was made of this in the referee's report and no complaint made by Dundee who, after all, had pocketed two points to get off to a good start.

On the same evening at Dens, Dundee's reserves ran out 7-2 winners against Falkirk with a side which included Craig Brown, George Ryden, Alex Stuart, George McGeachie, Bobby Waddell and Tommy Mackle. All would make their mark at first-team level for Dundee.

On the Saturday it was back to the League Cup, which now alternated with league fixtures so that matches came thick and fast. Four players – Hamilton, Cox, Cousin, and Robertson – had never been allowed to forget Dundee's 1-7 thrashing at Airdrie in December 1957. Every time they returned to Broomfield it was with revenge in mind, and a 5-0 win helped them sleep easy. Once again Smith was the man who lit the fuse, scoring Dundee's second goal direct from a free-kick, and placing crosses onto Gilzean's head for the fourth and fifth.

Despite the one-sided score, Airdrie had had their moments, and Ian Ure in particular took the eye when the ball was at the wrong end of the pitch. The following Monday he was named, along with Gilzean, in the Scottish League squad to face the League of Ireland in September.

Rangers had already qualified for the quarter-finals by the time they came to Dens on 30 August. A crowd of 24,000 was enticed out to see Gordon Smith make his competitive home debut, having scored in all of Dundee's last three away games. Meaningless in terms of results, the Rangers clash was nevertheless a thriller. 'Shug' Robertson netted after three minutes, but Ralph Brand equalised. Importantly, Dundee showed yet again that they could compete with Rangers, and this time earned a more positive result than at Ibrox. It was the only point Rangers would drop in their six League Cup sectional ties.

Less praiseworthy were those Dundee fans who invaded the pitch when Shug scored. Encroaching onto the playing surface was beginning to become a habit for the Dundee supporters during big games. The culprits tended mostly to be young boys, but there was also an increasing trend for young adults to join in, and the club was keen to nip the problem in the bud.

The pitch at Dens was fairly accessible for the support. It was close to the terracing, and the perimeter wall behind the goals was only waist-high for a young teen, and so could be easily surmounted. On the other hand, the terracing on the south side enclosure and underneath the main stand was constructed so that the lower steps were well below pitch level. Consequently, as the wall extended up to the waist of an adult, it acted as more a deterrent to anyone wanting to jump onto the track. The majority of boys who invaded the pitch did so from behind the goals, from where they could more easily get over the wall. And because crowds were generally large, most youngsters stood at the perimeter wall, where they didn't have to struggle to see over an adult.

Fans had run onto the pitch on a number occasions the previous season. As the Rangers League Cup-tie was only the second home fixture of the new season, the club was determined to try to crack down. At the next home game, against Third Lanark, it was announced over the tannoy that fans must not run onto the pitch under any circumstances. The announcer was wasting his time, for it was a meaningless League Cup-tie that had little to get excited about. The crowd was down by two thirds on the Rangers visit and Thirds scored their second equaliser in the dying moments. The *Courier* suggested the game revived memories of 1948-49. Then, the Cathkin Park side had scored a dubious last-gasp equaliser in December to deprive Dundee of a point – and that point was the difference between winning and losing the championship. This time it meant nothing. Dundee finished five points behind Rangers.

Any disappointment the players felt in not qualifying for the quarter-finals was tempered for some by their inclusion in the Scotland squad to face Czechoslovakia in a World Cup qualifier. Hamilton, Seith, Ure, and Gilzean were all named in the squad, from which the team would be announced later in September.

The 61-62 season would see three Dundee players – Alex Hamilton, Ian Ure and Hugh Robertson – all gain full Scottish caps. Hamilton, the most capped player in the club's history, lined up against England, Wales, Uruguay and Czechoslovakia, not to mention gaining Scottish League caps against the Italian and English Leagues. Ure was picked to play against Wales and Czechoslovakia, as well as the League of Ireland and the Italian League. Robertson was chosen against the Auld Enemy and Czechoslovakia. The Czech play-off decider in November in Brussels was the only occasion in the twentieth century in which three Dundee players lined up in the same Scotland side.

Gilzean had to wait until 1964 for his full Scottish debut, but played in 1961-62 for the Under-23 Scottish side against England and Wales and for the Scottish League against the League of Ireland. Penman earned his second Under-23 cap that season against Wales.

There was recognition, too, for Dundee director Jack Swadel, who was presented with a long-service medal by the SFA. Swadel currently served on the SFA's finance committee, but he had started out serving as treasurer, vice president, and then president on the Second XI's committee. Swadel then moved after four years to the senior body, where he served for the next seven years in several capacities, including the international select committee.

With the League Cup sections done, the first midweek in September was the first break Dundee had enjoyed since the start of the season. But not for Ian Ure and Alan Gilzean, who lined up for the Scottish League against the League of Ireland. The rest of the team prepared for the biggest game of the season so far, the visit of neighbours Dundee United. The game was eagerly anticipated locally, and had added spice owing to United having finished the 1960-61 season above the Dark Blues for the first time ever.

United's emergence had acted as a wake-up call to Dundee. Hugh Taylor in the *Daily Record* suggested that 'it spurred Dundee into jogging them out of the local complacency they could often fall into'. Dundee had never lost to United in the league at Dens, and didn't intend doing so in the first derby of the season.

In the decades before United shook themselves into life, supporters in the city had often gone to watch Dundee one week and United the next. Dundee fans historically felt more sympathy for, than resentment against their local rivals. As Dundee became successful in the early 1950s and started winning trophies, United felt that their rivals had adopted a 'superior attitude' and they would enjoy trying to knock them down to size whenever the two clubs faced each other in the Scottish Cup, League Cup or Forfarshire Cup.

Rangers and Celtic undoubtedly supply the greatest club rivalry in Scotland, but its dark side often leaves a nasty taste. This cannot be said about the partisanship that exists between Dundee and Dundee United fans who, next to the Old Firm, provide Scotland's greatest rivals. Indeed, Dundee United programme editor Peter Rundo describes the relationship between the two clubs as 'healthy rivalry, which compares more with the competition that exists on Merseyside between Liverpool and Everton, which is full of divided families who can live in harmony, rather than the acrid antithesis that exists between Old Firm factions.'

In May 1999, on the eve of Dundee's 2-0 win at Tannadice, which confirmed Dundee's first league finish above United in 25 years, club captain Barry Smith described the local rivalry as 'the best in Scotland'. Having played for Celtic against Rangers before he signed for Dundee, Smith was well placed to make a judgment.

By 1961 that local rivalry had reached such intensity that many fans no longer watched the other side when their own was playing away. In the *Courier*, former Dundee player Tommy Gallacher pointed out that, 'Dundonians would prefer to watch the reserves, who would play the second string of the side they were away to that day at home, in preference to even the best opposition across the road.' He added: 'Come Saturday there were few in the city who would pretend neutrality,' and he recalled how much he used to enjoy beating Dundee United when he played for Dundee between 1947 and 1956. 'Apart from the possibility of beating Glasgow's big two, I know from experience there is no greater thrill than a victory over local opposition.'

Former United players said much the same. A typical reaction came from former Dundee United stalwart Davie Dorward, who had been domiciled in Canada for fifteen years after playing wing-half for the

Tannadice club when they won the Second Division championship in 1928-29. Dorward had been invited back home to attend a niece's wedding. When he heard that the latest local derby was scheduled a week beforehand, he arranged to fly home a week early, hoping to see United put one over the Dees.

Dundee fan Derek Burgess recalls that the atmosphere at derbies around this time was 'electric and generated an air of excitement which seemed to bring out the best in both teams'. With supporters of both clubs generally starved of local derbies, thanks to United's exile in the lower tier, the build up to the game reached fever pitch. A 20,000 crowd turned up at Dens, with home fans hoping that Dundee could go one better than the 3-0 win in the corresponding fixture last season. No one of a Dark Blue persuasion was disappointed as Dundee romped to a 4-1 win. Dundee ripped holes in the United defence with their short passing game and pacy attack.

Andy Penman opened the scoring with his third goal in four games against United, and Gordon Smith scored his first goal at Dens. United full-back Johnny Briggs netted an unfortunate own-goal to make it 3-0 before Gillespie pulled one back before half-time. United, playing in white, (they only changed to tangerine in 1969) conceded a fourth, scored by Robertson, before the end. The final score, 4-1, marked Dundee's biggest league victory over United since 1926.

That weekend NASA expressed fears that the Soviet Union had put a second man in space, following Yuri Gagarin earlier in the year. But what were thought to be transmissions from a new Russian launch was perhaps just the cheers from the home crowd at Dens. Having got their indifferent League Cup form out of their system, Dundee's league quest had started positively. Dundee and Rangers shared the lead with maximum points from two matches.

September saw the launch in Scotland of Grampian Television, a new independent television channel to serve the north-east of Scotland. Based in Aberdeen, Grampian transmitted into the north and immediate south of the Granite City, encompassing Dundee and its surroundings. Scottish Television was already established as an independent television channel, but its emphasis was on Glasgow and Edinburgh. Dundee could now look forward to local news and features from the new station. Grampian pledged to introduce more native songs, traditions, artists and speech, and its launch coincided with Dundee's league visit to Pittodrie to face Aberdeen.

Although Scottish Television transmitted a Saturday night programme called 'Scotsport', Grampian's schedule did not at that time allow it, so the viewers in Aberdeen and Dundee were denied their independent TV Scottish football highlights.

'Scotsport' became a television institution in Scotland. It was hosted by popular presenter Arthur Montford and his famous tweed sports jackets. Montford, who hosted the show for over 30 years, once described Dundee's title-winning side as 'the best club side ever to come out of Scotland'. But the launch of Grampian TV meant that Dundonians could not watch that great side on television on Saturday nights whenever they featured. Instead, viewers were treated to the likes of Perry Mason on BBC if the 'native' programmes weren't to suit.

It's a shame that the Aberdeen v Dundee match didn't feature on the new TV channel as it had everything – four goals, controversial decisions, and dazzling skill. Sadly for Dundee the dazzling skill didn't come from anyone in Dark Blue. The star was a future Dee, Charlie Cooke.

Cooke would sign for Dundee from Aberdeen in December 1964 for £40,000, then leave for Chelsea two years later for £72,000. Cooke was a sublime winger who would ably replace Gilzean when he left for Spurs, but on 16 September 1961 Cooke's concoction of ball skills and wizardry outshone Dundee's golden boy. Aberdeen ran out 3-1 winners to inflict on Dundee their first league defeat of the season. Charlie Cooke was involved in all three Dons goals. The first came from the spot after his cross was allegedly handled by Hamilton. Dundee would later head south burning with a sense of injustice over the incident that had turned the game. But Dundee had got their tactics wrong from the start, trying to play precise football at a fast pace in the face of a blustery wind which often dogs games at Pittodrie.

Gilzean's goal came at a time when his team were three goals down. Dundee's first league defeat saw them slip to sixth, with Aberdeen now third and Rangers still top despite dropping their first point in a 2-2 draw at home to Celtic.

Despite the result, the press once again commended Ian Ure's performance. The consensus was that centre-half was his natural position, not the left-half slot he had previously filled. Ure had broken into the first team at left-half by the end of his second season at Dens, but the signing of Burnley's Bobby Seith meant that Ure returned to the reserves with little chance, he thought, of a quick return. With veteran Doug Cowie established on the other flank, it looked like the youngster from Ayr was destined for a lengthy spell in the second XI, but a couple of twists of football fortune changed the path of Ure's career.

Ure's first big break came when Cowie took ill and Ure was chosen to play for the first team in the pre-season trial of 1960. He did well enough to be picked to play against Valenciennes of France in the Anglo-French Cup. (This was a two-legged tie which Bobby Cox remembers as giving Dundee vital European experience.) Ure did not look out of place in either leg and kept his place when the league season started. A second turn of fate then cemented his footballing future. Midway through the season centre-half Billy Smith was injured and Ure was moved across to cover for him, performing so well that by the end of 1960-61 his place as the regular pivot was secure.

The signing of inside-left Bobby Wishart in January 1961 meant that Ure would become the middle man between two fine half-backs. Ure described himself as 'the legs between the Seith and Wishart, who were the old heads and creative parts of the machine', while he became 'the mobile one, the hit man between them.'

The press, locally and nationally, began to recognise this and conjectured that Ure was better suited to centre-half. The Scottish League selectors seemed to agree, naming Ure after the Aberdeen game on the reserve list for the Scottish League's forthcoming match against the Irish League. It was the start of an international path that for Ure would take in eleven full caps for Scotland and four Scottish League caps.

Against Aberdeen, the Seith-Ure-Wishart half-back line had been disrupted by injury to Wishart. Alec Stuart took his place, but against Hearts the following week Wishart was back in his normal place. Gordon Smith looked forward to returning to Tynecastle, an old stomping ground, but he was a fitness doubt right up until kick-off because of boils on his backside. Smith declared himself fit to play, however, and for Dundee it was a stroke of good fortune as Smith reminded his old club what they were missing.

Dundee lined up in their white change kit to avoid a clash with Hearts' maroon, even though it was usual in Scotland at the time for the home team to change. In 1961-62 Dundee wore all white at Dens whenever welcoming Rangers, Raith, St Johnstone, Hearts and Falkirk.

Gilzean's knee was at last healed, and he was the key man, scoring his first league double after swapping positions with Alan Cousin as part of of Shankly's tactical switch. This time last year Gillie had scored fourteen goals, compared to four this term. Dundee were up to second, behind Rangers on goal-average but ahead of Kilmarnock, also on the same points. Airdrie had beaten Dundee's previous conquerors, Aberdeen, 7-1 which, considering the Dees had whipped Airdrie 5-0 in the League Cup, put that wretched defeat at Pittodrie into perspective.

That month the city's first multi-storey flats were going up in the area of Drybrough. Lord Provost McManus described them as symbolic of the new Dundee. Perhaps more symbolic of the 'new Dundee' was the Dark Blues' high rise in the League table. To maintain their good start, the Dees now had to overcome Third Lanark, whom they had twice failed to beat in the League Cup. Ure was doubtful. Like Gordon Smith, he now had trouble with boils. If he was ruled out, who would replace him at Cathkin Park? The choice seemed to lie between Billy McMillan – the regular reserve centre-half – or Billy Smith, who had been the established pivot before Ure broke through, but was now playing wing-half in the second XI. In the event, come matchday, Ure declared himself fit.

An unchanged Dundee showed their mettle, brushing aside a team that had earlier caused them problems. Gilzean scored his second double in two weeks – both goals were headers from Bobby Seith crosses – to seal Dundee's 3-1 win.

October saw Helen Shapiro top the UK music charts with 'Walkin' Back To Happiness'. Dundee were themselves walking (or playing, even) to happiness by also going to the top of the own chart. October 7th, 1961, was the date when the Dees hit the top of Division One for the first time in twelve years. It was down to a thrilling performance and a fantastic result. Dundee knew beforehand that if they overcame third-placed Kilmarnock they would go top because leaders Rangers were inactive. Scotland were due to play Northern Ireland in Belfast the same afternoon (Scotland won 6-1) and, with four Gers players called up, their league fixture was postponed. Internationals were played concurrently with league matches at that time, and the English and Scottish national sides had first pick on players. This frequently led to the affected clubs requesting postponements.

No greater incentive was therefore required, and Dundee ended the day 5-3 winners over fancied Killie. The performance showed determination, skill and character. The Dens Park crowd went home happy, having seen their heroes score eleven goals in three home league games. For Andy Penman, the game had special significance. He scored a hat-trick against a side against whom he broke an ankle last season. His only previous hat-trick had come against Hibs in March 1960.

In the 1962 *Scotsport Football Annual,* Alex Cameron wrote: 'Dundee's play is in contrast to many of the other teams in Scotland, whose passes come at such speed that the players for whom they are intended have to worry more about getting the ball under control than about being in a position to shoot. The supply to the Dundee forwards is often immaculate and they in turn are often in perfect balance as well in a perfect position when they shoot and this was never more amply demonstrated than in their win over Kilmarnock at Dens Park in October.'

The showing against Kilmarnock was carried on against Motherwell, in a match which Bob Shankly described as 'our finest all round display of the season'. Like Kilmarnock, Motherwell were considered one of the better footballing side in Scotland. Managed by Bobby Ancell – who would replace Bob Shankly in the Dundee hot seat in 1965 – they played a fast attacking game and were hard to beat at Fir Park. Dundee, however, kept their momentum going with another sackful of goals, sparked by Penman's first-minute penalty. Dundee ran out winners by 4-2.

Back-to-back wins over Kilmarnock and Motherwell, coupled with an average of three goals per game, made many sceptics sit up and take notice. Journalist Bob Crampsey was even moved to 'invest heavily' on Dundee, laying out £10 for the Dees to win the league at odds greatly reduced from the start of the season.

Rangers, though, kept up the pressure by thrashing Raith Rovers 6-0. The scheduled clash between the big two in November was already being circled in diaries and calendars, but there were three other games to complete before minds could turn to that potential showdown. Dunfermline were going well in the European Cup-Winners' Cup, Partick were themselves riding high in the top six, as indeed were Celtic.

Dunfermline were managed by the then comparatively unknown Jock Stein. They had lifted the Scottish Cup with a 2-0 replay win over Celtic and had already progressed to the second round in Europe. The Pars, playing at home, would therefore provide Dundee with a stiff test if they hoped to extend their unbeaten run to five matches. Their cause was not helped by an injury to Gordon Smith in the first minute. As was customary in those pre-substitute days, the injured player stayed on, hobbling up and down the touchline out of harm's way, offering nuisance value only. When Hamilton's foul on Melrose allowed the Pars to net from the spot, Dundee's second defeat looked on the cards, but a second-half turnaround earned a 2-1 victory. Shankly doubtless allowed himself a smile when hearing that Rangers had dropped a point at Fir Park. Dundee's lead was extended to three points, though Rangers had a game in hand.

	P	W	D	L	F	A	Pts
Dundee	8	7	0	1	24	12	14
Rangers	7	4	3	0	22	7	11
Partick	8	5	1	2	18	14	11
Kilmarnock	8	5	1	2	20	16	11

The following week Dundee had the chance to widen their lead to five points as Rangers were again inactive, taking on Hearts in the League Cup final at Hampden. In Dundee's path were Partick Thistle who themselves were having a decent campaign, lying third. They too hoped to profit from Rangers' inactivity. Partick had a good recent record at Dens and in the corresponding fixture the previous season had beaten Dundee 2-1.

Shankly made one change from the side which had rattled off five straight wins. Gordon Smith had failed to recover and in his place came George McGeachie for his first match since the League Cup defeat at Ibrox. In the early stages Dundee appeared to miss Smith's positioning, passing and crossing, and Gilzean and Cousin struggled to find their rhythm. Thistle scored early and it took Dundee half an hour to create their first chance, which Alan Cousin took. Penman then put his team ahead from the spot after he had been fouled by Hogan. Now that Doug Cowie had left the club, Penman was the regular penalty taker. This was his fourth successful kick and Andy was finding himself dubbed by the fans the 'Penalty King'. Partick made it 2-2 from a set-piece, and it was not until two minutes from time that Penman fired the winner. A five-point lead had been secured over Rangers and Partick, while Kilmarnock went clear in second place, three points behind Dundee. Celtic now moved into fourth on the same points as Rangers.

Celtic at this time were overshadowed by their Old Firm rivals. They hadn't won the League since 1953-54, the Scottish Cup likewise, and had not lifted the League Cup since they beat Rangers 7-1 in 1957. In other words, Celtic had won only one trophy in seven years. By comparison, in that same period Rangers had raised the League flag four times, the Scottish Cup once, and the League Cup twice. Celtic were in transition and, like Dundee, were trying to bring through young players. Their current team already had McNeill, Clark, Chalmers and Lennox in place, all of whom would all be immortalised six years later as part of the Lisbon Lions.

The city of Dundee has a large Celtic following, stemming from the nineteenth-century influx of Irish. In percentage terms, Dundee had more Irish immigrants than either Glasgow or Liverpool, and so the city built up a large support for Celtic from those who wished to support a club with Irish or Catholic roots instead of a local side. Dundee United had been founded in 1909 as Dundee Hibernian in an attempt to provide a sporting focal point for the Irish population in the city, but in 1923 they changed their name to Dundee United in an attempt to distance themselves from Irish or Catholic associations. (The name Hibernian comes from the Latin word for Ireland, Hibernia.) This naturally served to reinforce support for the Glasgow Irish club in Dundee. Areas such as the Hilltown and Lochee had thriving Celtic supporters clubs in the early

1960s and ran buses to Parkhead. In fact, the Dundee Celtic Supporters Club is still based in the Hilltown today. Therefore, whenever Celtic come to Dens Park or Tannadice they are assured of a large support, many of whom are Dundonians.

On 4 November, 1961, Celtic travelled to Dens without injured Scotland centre-half Billy McNeill. Dundee were boosted by the news that Gordon Smith was fit. Dundee had failed to beat Celtic home or away last season and needed to improve on that if their growing title credentials were not to be undermined.

The match was an end-to-end thriller. Carroll equalised Wishart's early goal before half-time, then Gilzean nodded a Cousin head-flick past Frank Haffey to give Dundee a vital 2-1 win. Dundee's patient approach had got the better of Celtic's 'up and at 'em tactics' and the experienced heads of Smith, Wishart and Seith were crucial in keeping Celtic at bay in the closing minutes. Behind them, Ian Ure was again immense and the victory was one of the highlights of a great season.

As the top six were all playing each other, something was bound to give. With Killie beating Partick, and Rangers defeating Third Lanark, it was the top three who pulled away from the rest. Dundee still held a three-point lead over Kilmarnock and a five-point lead over Rangers, who they were due to face next at Ibrox.

For the moment, there were the repercussions from the Celtic match to consider. With a sizeable Celtic support in the 24,500 Dens crowd, the match was marred by crowd trouble inside the ground and afterwards in the city centre, where a riot ensued.

Dundee as a club did not have a history of crowd trouble, and over the years incidents at Dens had been few and far between. At the Celtic match, however, supporters of both sides ran onto the pitch when their team scored, and order had to be restored before the game could resume. The police had to make one arrest beforehand as the biggest crowd of the season so far converged on Dens, and during it they made four more arrests. The police complained in the *Sunday Post* the following day of 'continued rowdyism throughout the ninety minutes'. Several spectators had to be taken away by ambulance. Some had fainted and a couple had vomited, while one Dundee fan had to be treated for a head wound after he was struck by a flying beer can.

This was nothing, however, compared to the trouble in the city centre that night. Eight pubs had to be closed before 8pm as violence erupted. Enraged at their team losing to Dundee, gangs of visiting Celtic fans rampaged through the streets, chanting and shouting, and police ended up making 25 arrests for drunkenness and breaches of the peace.

The worst affected areas were south of the centre in Dock Street, where fights broke out between rival sets of supporters. Rival fans also clashed in Union Street, High Street and in the Overgate. By 11pm, 60 Celtic supporters' buses were still parked along Riverside Drive with many of their occupants engaged in trouble-making elsewhere. The Dundee police described it as the worst night of trouble in the history of the city.

The trouble seemed to have been sparked as early as 6pm. The landlord of the City Centre Bar in Dock Street described how a group of about 30 Celtic supporters entered his bar with an accordion and launched into 'community signing'. Unable to hear the orders of other customers, he asked the Celtic fans to leave. When they refused he called the police to remove them. Their arrival sparked a 'riot'. Glasses and chairs were thrown over the bar and similar stories were reported across the city. One bar had its front door knocked in and another had its plate glass window smashed.

Thirty men were taken to Dundee Royal Infirmary during the course of the night to be treated for cuts and lacerations and, on the Monday, licensees in Dundee met to demand that police should be given wider powers to escort visiting supporters out of the city as soon as the match was finished.

The build up to the impending Rangers clash was somewhat overshadowed by the events of the previous weekend, but by the end of the week, sights were clearly focused on what was probably Dundee's biggest league match in twelve years. Such was the interest throughout Scotland that, on the Friday night, Dundee full-backs Alex Hamilton and Bobby Cox were interviewed by Arthur Montford for the STV topical programme 'Here and Now'. When asked about Dundee's prospects at Ibrox, Hamilton said 'we should have nothing to fear', while Cox was confident that the team could continue their recent good run.

When Montford asked Cox about Dundee's championship prospects, the player replied: 'It's a bit early but everyone is pulling their weight and it'll take a good team to beat us.' In reply to a question about Dundee's forwards gaining all the credit, Hammy replied: 'As long as we get the goals, we don't care who gets the credit.'

Confidence was obviously high in the Dundee camp but the Rangers match on 11 November was undoubtedly a huge challenge. The Ibrox club boasted seven internationalists in their line up and were unbeaten in 21 games. They already had this season's League Cup in the bag, having beaten Hearts 3-1 in a replayed final. They were also clear favourites for the title, despite being five points behind their opponents.

A huge crowd was expected to descend upon Ibrox, with over a thousand intending to make the journey from Dundee. British Rail ran a football special from Dundee West Station to Buchanan Street in Glasgow for a cost of fifteen shillings (75p), compared to the regular fare of 19s 3d (96p), and Dicksons Coaches in Reform Street ran buses to the game for a cost of 12s 6d (62½p).

On matchday however, Glasgow was shrouded in fog and rumours circulated quickly that the game had been postponed. The weather forecast had been for the fog to clear by midday and, when it didn't, numerous Dundee supporters' buses were turned away by police less than a mile from the ground. My father's bus was among those prematurely turned back, and he always said that missing one of the greatest results in the club's history pained him to such an extent that he vowed it would never happen to him again.

Twelve years later, in December 1973, Dundee faced Celtic in the League Cup final at Hampden. Confronted by a miners' strike and a national energy crisis, the authorities scheduled the game to kick off at 1.30pm to avoid the necessity for floodlights. For days, blizzards had raged around Scotland and the game was in serious jeopardy. After driving for three hours from Dundee to Glasgow (a journey which would normally take an hour), my dad was met a few miles from Mount Florida by police, who told him the game was off.

Remembering his experience in 1961, he was determined to proceed to Hampden anyway, to check for himself, and was glad he did. The game went ahead and Dundee won 1-0 in front of 29,974, the lowest ever crowd for a Hampden final, and one wonders how many others were deterred by bogus information given by the police.

Those who travelled by train in 1961 were luckier than those who went by road. The football specials which left Dundee at 11.30am arrived in Glasgow at 1.45pm. With the return train not due to depart until 6.30pm, the majority of Dundee supporters made their way to the ground expecting to twiddle their thumbs for four hours. They were delighted and ultimately fortunate to find that the game was still on.

The worst of the fog cleared half an hour before kick-off. It was only then that the referee decided that the game should go ahead. A crowd of only 38,000, roughly half of the Ibrox capacity, went through the turnstiles. Had it not been for the fog and the rumours of postponement, Ibrox would have been crammed to the gills.

Dundee lined up at full strength. With a record of three wins and a draw in the last four league meetings at Ibrox, they fancied their chances, especially as they were on a seven-game winning run. Visibility was still poor on the terracing, but the game kicked off on time at 3pm. Forty-five minutes later it was still goalless, but Rangers' Jim Baxter was running the show. At half-time Shankly ordered Penman to adopt a more attacking stance, so that Baxter would be forced to track back. The tactical change paid immediate dividends when Gilzean finished off a move involving Penman and Cousin by heading past Ritchie in the Rangers goal.

Within seconds Gilzean added a second but, worryingly, the fog was returning. Visibility had deteriorated to such an extent that Pat Liney in the Dundee goal didn't know that his team was 2-0 up until skipper Cox shouted back to him as the players lined up to restart.

If the score was a treat, it was about to get even better. Gilzean completed his hat-trick and, although Ralph Brand pulled one back for Rangers, Gilzean immediately thundered in his fourth. To score four goals at Ibrox is the measure of any player, and Gilzean duly established himself as a fully-fledged Dundee hero. Nor were the Dark Blues finished, for Andy Penman completed the rout with a fifth goal, and all five had been scored in the second half. Rangers' unbeaten record in all competitions had been obliterated.

The final score of 5-1 to Dundee is untouchable as the greatest league result in the history of the club. It was a famous victory in the swirling Govan fog and those who were fortunate enough to witness it and ignore the rumours of postponement were the envy of Dundee fans everywhere. With Dundee's defence superbly marshalled by Ure in the first half, and the forwards rampant in the second, the team showed that their championship challenge had to be taken seriously.

	P	W	D	L	F	A	Pts
Dundee	11	10	0	1	34	15	20
Rangers	9	5	3	1	26	12	13
Hearts	10	6	1	3	20	13	13
Kilmarnock	11	7	1	3	28	21	13

Dundee were now seven points ahead of the defending champions (who had two games in hand), but they now had the belief that they were good enough to lift the flag. Shankly had always believed in his side, but the rest of the country was coming round to the view that he might have prospective champions at Dens Park. Rangers had in recent years been the team to stop but now, almost a third of the way through the campaign, Dundee were clear of the pack.

Hugh Robertson gives Dundee the lead at home to Rangers in a League Cup-tie in August 1961. The game ended 1-1 and Rangers qualified from the group

Preparing for the Great Leap Forward – Bobby Wishart jumps over Bobby Cox during pre-season training at Dens Park in July 1961

Alan Gilzean jumps with St Mirren goalkeeper Brown at Dens Park in the penultimate game of the 1961-62 season. Dundee won 2-0

Bobby Cox waves from the City Chambers balcony to the Dundee fans assembled in the City Square below – the evening of Saturday, 28 April 1962

Andy Penman heads Dundee's sixth goal past a stand-in goalkeeper in this 8-1 thrashing of Cologne in the European Cup – September 1962

Dundee come back from 0-2 down against Raith Rovers to win 5-4. Gordon Smith is swamped by his team-mates after hitting the winner – November 1961

Alan Gilzean heads the first of his two goals against Clyde at Shawfield – January 1963

The Dundee squad line up with the Scottish Championship trophy at the start of the 1962-63 season

The author, Kenny Ross, with Championship skipper Bobby Cox

Dundee captain Alfie Boyd shows fans the League Cup at Buchanan Street Station, Glasgow, after Dundee had become the first club to retain the trophy – October 1953

Alan Gilzean beats Rangers' Harold Davis to the ball and heads past Billy Ritchie to open the scoring in Dundee's 5-1 win at Ibrox – November 1961

Penman, arms raised, celebrates Alan Gilzean's winner in the 2-1 triumph over Dundee United at Tannadice in April 1962. Gilzean, far left, is hugged by Robertson

Alan Gilzean leaps to congratulate Andy Penman, who has just scored Dundee's third goal at St Johnstone to clinch the League Championship – April 1962

History in the making. Dundee and Cologne line up for the national anthems in the first ever European Cup-tie at Dens Park. Dundee won 8-1 – September 1962

Andy Penman scores from the penalty spot past Rangers' Billy Ritchie in a 1-1 Scottish Cup draw at Dens Park – March 1963

Alan Gilzean helps out in defence by clearing off the line as Anderlecht pile on the pressure in the European Cup quarter-final at Dens – March 1963

Gilzean challenges AC Milan keeper Ghezzi in the European Cup semi-final, second leg at Dens Park in May 1963. Gilzean scored the only goal of the night, but was also sent off

Dundee show off the League Cup at Dens Park, a week after winning their first trophy in 42 years – October 1952

Hugh Robertson, on the ground, awaits Dundee trainer Sammy Kean, who is running on (third right) with the magic sponge. Dundee beat Kilmarnock 5-3 – October 1961

Billy Steel, one of Dundee's greatest ever players. He signed in September 1950 for a world record fee of £23,500

Dundee's record scorer, 'Gillie' prepares to take on Falkirk at Dens in January 1962. He scores twice, wearing sandshoes

Sandshoe shuffle. Alan Gilzean scores his first goal and Dundee's second in a 2-1 home win over Falkirk at a frozen Dens Park – January 1962

An airborne Alan Gilzean opens the scoring on Dundee's glory day at St Johnstone in April 1962. Defeat meant that St Johnstone were relegated

The match programme for St Johnstone v Dundee, 28 April 1962. Dundee won 3-0 to claim the Scottish League title

Ian Ure was a giant at the heart of the Dundee defence, here defending against Dundee United at Dens – August 1963

Champagne Charlies! Dundee players celebrate outside Muirton Park, Perth, after winning the Scottish League title, April 1962

Sporting heroes. Alan Gilzean shakes hands with Cologne defender Benthaus as Dundee applaud the German team off at Dens after their 8-1 win – September 1962

Ian Ure prepares to launch the ball upfield on the muddy surface against Anderlecht in the European Cup quarter-final second leg – March 1963

Bob Shankly, left, who led Dundee to the semi-final of the European Cup in 1963, with Jock Stein, who went one better, winning the trophy with Celtic in 1967

Dundee FC match programme for the 4-1 derby win over Dundee United, September 1961. The photograph on the front is taken from the corner of the Provost Road and Dens Road terracing, and was used on programme covers from the mid-1950s until 1966

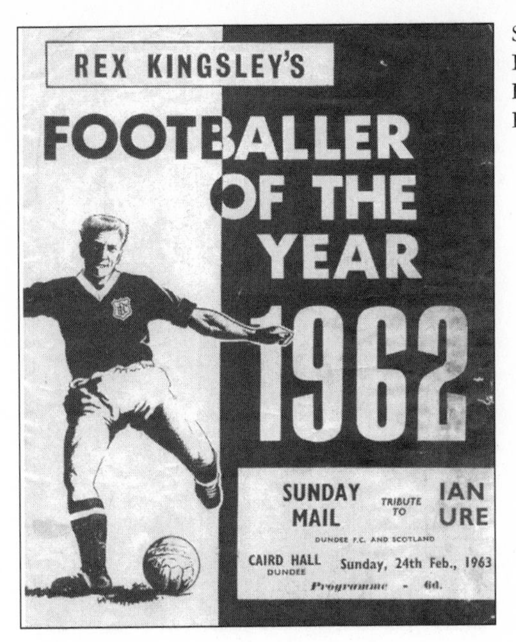

Souvenir programme to celebrate Ian Ure being voted Scottish Footballer of the Year, 1962, by Rex Kingsley of the *Sunday Mail*

Players on a pre-season route march at the top of Provost Road, near Dens Park, July 1956. The players at the front are Merchant, Cowie, Brown, Irvine and coach MacAuley

Gordon Smith spins away towards Alan Cousin after Smith scores Dundee's second goal past Dundee United keeper Ugolini in a 4-1 home win – September 1961

Dundee players protest. Referee Brittle has awarded a corner after Shanks fisted the ball away at Broomfield. Brittle consults a linesman and changes his mind – April 1962

Dundee fans in good voice as they prepare for the biggest game of their lives, at Muirton Park, April 1962

A sea of joy. Dundee supporters engulf Bobby Cox on the pitch after the final whistle. Dundee have beaten St Johnstone at Muirton to be crowned Champions of Scotland

Cologne keeper Fritz Ewart is out cold after colliding with Alan Cousin in the second minute at Dens. Ewart was replaced at half-time and Cologne played on with ten men

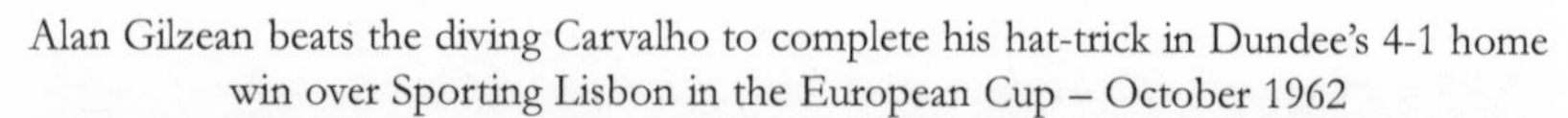

Alan Gilzean beats the diving Carvalho to complete his hat-trick in Dundee's 4-1 home win over Sporting Lisbon in the European Cup – October 1962

Dens Park as it looked in 1962. This view, from the east, overlooks the Dens Road, South Enclosure, with the city's extinct volcano, The Law, in the background

Bobby Seith, right, captains Dundee in the absence of Bobby Cox for the second leg of the European Cup semi-final v Milan. Seith won the toss but Dundee were eliminated

Penman, No 8, pats Gilzean on the head after he had scored the winning goal at Dens past Celtic keeper Frank Haffey, November 1961. The match sparked riots

Dundee players celebrate Alan Gilzean's second goal at St Johnstone in April 1962, to put Dundee well on the way to securing their first League championship

European heroes – full-backs Alex Hamilton and Bobby Cox are behind Craig Brown and goalkeeper Bert Slater, who would excel in the 1962-63 European Cup campaign

Alan Gilzean fires past Cologne goalkeeper Ewart for the first goal of his hat-trick in Dundee's 8-1 demolition of Cologne at Dens Park – September 1962

Dundee players prepare to fly from London Airport to face Sporting Lisbon in the European Cup. Dundee lost that first leg 0-1, but won at home 4-1 – October 1962

Alan Gilzean beats AC Milan's Benitez to score the only goal in the European Cup semi-final second leg at Dens Park in May 1963. Dundee went out 2-5 on aggregate

Trainer Reggie Smith (left), manager George Anderson (centre) and assistant trainer Reuben Bennett guided Dundee to three Hampden cup finals in the early 1950s

Dundee skipper Bobby Cox cradles the Scottish League Championship trophy in August 1962

Ian Ure is interviewed at Dens by Marcel de Leener for Belgian television, prior to the second leg of the European Cup quarter-final against Anderlecht – March 1963

Bob Shankly in the stand at Falkirk during Dundee's first league game of their championship campaign

The match programme for Dundee's greatest ever league result – a 5-1 win at Rangers in November 1961

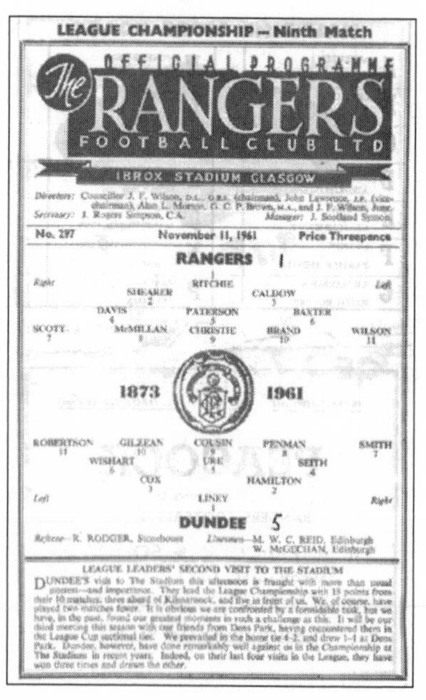

LEAGUE CHAMPIONSHIP – Ninth Match

OFFICIAL PROGRAMME

The RANGERS FOOTBALL CLUB LTD

IBROX STADIUM GLASGOW

Directors: Councillor J. F. Wilson, D.L., O.B.E. (chairman), John Lawrence, J.P. (vice-chairman), Alan L. Morton, G. C. P. Brown, M.A., and J. F. Wilson, Junr.
Secretary: J. Rogers Simpson, C.A. *Manager:* J. Scotland Symon

No. 297 November 11, 1961 Price Threepence

RANGERS 1

Right RITCHIE 1 *Left*
SHEARER 2 CALDOW 3
DAVIS 4 PATERSON 5 BAXTER 6
SCOTT 7 McMILLAN 8 CHRISTIE 9 BRAND 10 WILSON 11

1873 1961

ROBERTSON 11 GILZEAN 10 COUSIN 9 PENMAN 8 SMITH 7
WISHART 6 URE 5 SEITH 4
COX 3 HAMILTON 2
Left LINEY 1 *Right*

DUNDEE 5

Referee—R. RODGER, Stonehouse *Linesmen*—M. W. C. REID, Edinburgh; W. McGECHAN, Edinburgh

LEAGUE LEADERS' SECOND VISIT TO THE STADIUM

DUNDEE'S visit to The Stadium this afternoon is fraught with more than usual interest—and importance. They lead the League Championship with 18 points from their 10 matches: three ahead of Kilmarnock, and five in front of us. We, of course, have played two matches fewer. It is obvious we are confronted by a formidable task, but we have, in the past, found our greatest moments in such a challenge as this. It will be our third meeting this season with our friends from Dens Park, having encountered them in the League Cup sectional ties. We prevailed in the home tie 4-2, and drew 1-1 at Dens Park. Dundee, however, have done remarkably well against us in the Championship at The Stadium in recent years. Indeed, on their last four visits in the League, they have won three times and drawn the other.

Alan Gilzean is swamped by joyous team-mates after scoring his fourth goal in Dundee's 5-1 win at Ibrox in November 1961

Manager Bob Shankly embraces Gordon Smith at the final whistle against St Johnstone at Muirton Park in the greatest moment in Dundee's history

Chapter 4

~ Winter of Discontent ~

(November 1961 – March 1962)

Rangers 1 Dundee 5. The score reverberated round Scottish football. It demonstrated to everyone, according to Craig Brown, that 'Dundee meant business and as the season wore on, it became more evident that our position at the top of the table was no mere flash in the pan.'

With regard to Ian Ure, that result also underlined Shankly's tactical genius. At half-time the match had been goalless and precariously balanced. According to Ure, 'Jim Baxter was the man who made Rangers tick and Bob was concerned with the space that was given to Baxter in the first half. Bob at half-time therefore told Andy Penman to man-mark Baxter in the second half but although Andy was a fantastic player and one of the most skilful I have ever seen, he couldn't tackle for toffee. The ploy worked a treat, however, as Andy would sit close to Baxter, deny him space and wouldn't fall for any of his tricks and shimmies, and we went on to score five in the second half when we looked liked scoring every time we went up the park!'

In Tuesday's *Courier*, 'Grandpa' from Dunblane penned a poem to his heroes which was published in *Tommy's Postbag.* The Ibrox result, added Grandpa, had revived memories of the great Dundee sides of the past, whose success he felt was now going to be emulated by the current team. 'It brought back sweet memories for all the grandads of Dundee.' His poem was a reworking of the Scottish folk song *A Gordon For Me.*

'When I was a boy, I belonged to Dundee,
Therein lay my heart, it was so dear to me,
And after the school, all our pals we would meet,
Kicking a tin can all over the street,
We all paid our pennies to buy a big ball,
Forgot about homework, our theme was football,
We trained every night, although we were wee,
Our object in view was to play for Dundee.

It's Dundee for me, it's Dundee for me,
If your no' for Dundee, yer nae use to me,

The Rangers are braw and Celtic and a',
But the Dark Blues of Dundee,
Are the pride of them a'.

That's long, long ago and we're now far and wide,
We remember the day when we had beaten the Clyde,
The match was in April, the year nineteen and ten,
We cheered and we cheered Captain Lee's gallant men,
And here once again, with our present team,
The league and the cup I'm sure we shall see,
Then up wi' the bonnets o' bonnie Dundee.'

Ever the realist, Bob Shankly wasn't fully convinced about his side's championship potential until the following week, when more drama unfolded at home to Raith Rovers. In front of 15,000 fans who expected big things after the Rangers win, Dundee found themselves 2-4 down with only 27 minutes left against a side who were struggling next to bottom in the table.

It had been a topsy-turvy game. Raith led 1-0 at the break, but Gilzean's two goals in two minutes restored Dundee's advantage. There then followed five minutes of Dundee madness in which Rovers netted three times. The match had seen five goals in just thirteen second-half minutes. What transpired, however, was interpreted by Bobby Seith as a 'key moment' in the title-winning year. 'Dundee's never-say-die attitude, allied with our undoubted skill, was able to rescue a victory from the jaws of defeat.'

Bobby Wishart pulled a goal back with an unstoppable shot, but only four minutes remained on the clock when Seith uncorked another rocket to register one of his personal highlights that season. Even so, 4-4 would have been a dreadful result against Raith, so Gordon Smith's winner in the dying seconds ensured that the 'Gay Gordon' was mobbed by his team-mates as the fans streamed onto the pitch to celebrate.

For the second week in a row, Dundee had hit five goals. They were playing – as Jim Hendry wrote in a 21st anniversary Dundee v Aberdeen match programme in 1983, 'a brand of attacking football that carried all before them.'

At the end of the season Bob Shankly referred to the 5-4 win over Raith as his 'number one match' and said that 'Dundee's terrific fight and last-gasp winner are surely among the greatest feats recorded all season.' The win over Raith, coupled with the rout at Ibrox, finally convinced Shankly that he had potential champions in his charge.

Bobby Cox also referred to the Raith match as 'a great game'. 'Even at two goals down we didn't give up and never froze and the win was as important as the win at Ibrox for the belief it gave the players that we could go on to win the league.'

By this stage, Dundee had averaged 3.25 goals per game and, according to Gilzean, were a side whom Shankly encouraged to go forward and take teams on. 'Rangers were the team to beat in Scotland at the time but they were defensive while we were attack-minded. We had a good defence but were better going forward and were attack-minded like Celtic, who would go on to be the first British team to lift the European Cup five years later with an attacking style like Dundee's.'

The following Wednesday, Dundee continued their goalscoring spree in a friendly against Swedish champions Elfsborg Boras. The Swedish league season had just finished but Elfsborg were expected to present a stiff challenge. After all, Sweden had reached the final of the 1958 World Cup, where they lost 2-5 to Brazil.

The match ended 8-2 to Dundee and was a personal triumph for 18-year-old Andy Penman who scored five goals and had a hand in two more. With Scotland selector Hugh Nelson among the Dens Park crowd of 11,000, Penman booked himself a place in the Scotland Under-23 side to face Wales on 6 December. Looking back after the championship was secured in April, the Elfsborg match was described in the *Sporting Post* as 'the finest home performance of the season.' Dundee lined up: Liney, Hamilton, Cox, Seith, Ure, Wishart, McGeachie, Penman, Cousin, Gilzean, Robertson. Elfsborg's team was Haraldsson, Malberg, Olssen, Sandstrom, Lundell, Lindroth, Grahn, Larsson, Barrtholdsson, Petterson, Raberg.

Including the Elfsborg friendly, Dundee had stretched their winning sequence to ten games since that controversial loss at Pittodrie. Equally important, Shankly had established a regular line up which had been virtually unchanged over the last three months. The team had also scored eighteen goals in three games.

Dundee's favoured eleven was Pat Liney in goal, Alex Hamilton at right-back and Bobby Cox at left-back. Ian Ure was ever present at centre half and on either side of him were wing-halves Bobby Seith on the right and Bobby Wishart on the left. George Hamilton of Third Lanark notes that, unlike today, most Scottish sides in 1961 lined up with two wide players. On the right wing for Dundee was the effervescent Gordon Smith, while on the left was Hugh Robertson. Alan Cousin played through the middle at centre-forward and was supported on either side by inside-left Alan Gilzean and inside-right Andy Penman.

Between September and Christmas there were only two enforced changes to this line up, first when Gordon Smith was replaced by George McGeachie when injured against Partick, and second when McGeachie came in for Gilzean in December, when Gillie missed matches against Airdrie and St Mirren.

Daily Record sports editor Hugh Taylor, in assessing Dundee's championship win in *The Scottish Football Book No 8* in June 1962, described Dundee's play as 'refreshing'. 'In a season in which many Scottish team formations appeared to be something of a "vital statistic report", what with 4-2-4 and 3-3-4 and other amazing permutations, Dundee had only one gimmick – putting the ball in the back of the net. What was Dundee's real secret? One was undoubtedly their hard-working manager, Mr Bob Shankly, among the finest strategists in the game. Dundee too, had the solid basis of sound players and didn't need to dream up any fancy formation. Instead they relied on their own understanding of the game, ball control, teamwork and spirit.'

In January, Bob Shankly gave a fascinating insight into his thoughts on Dundee's approach in a interview with *The Scotsman* newspaper: 'You must play football as you see fit. When a side goes out it can have as many plans and Continental ideas as it wants but for the 90 minutes the team can only play as well as the opposition will allow. Hard training counts of course and we train very hard at Dens. With Sammy Kean in charge, we're as fit as any team and, before the match, we get together and talk over the match and the opposition. Of course, I can only tell my lads what to expect, using my experience and knowledge. But you must remember that the opposition are also studying Dundee and often change their style when they meet us. When that happens it is impossible for me to go onto the pitch and give a new tactics talk. The players must be intelligent enough to read the game as it goes on.'

Craig Brown, whom Shankly exalted almost as a deity – the manager would often start a sentence with 'Christ! Craig' – remembers that 'there was little or no time spent on tactics. The players themselves worked those out, and some of us used to stay behind after official training to plan a few things. The senior players, particularly right-half Bobby Seith, who had won the English League Championship with Burnley, would evolve the set pieces from throw-ins and free-kicks and we would practise these without supervision when the regular training had been completed. I would suggest that this was pretty unusual, not only then, but also now.'

Gilzean remembers that Shankly liked nothing complicated in the way his team went about their business on the park and remembers one time when he tried to wind up Gordon Smith he got a rebuke from Shankly for his pains. In the dressing room at half-time Smith was feeling exhausted. Gillie jested to Shankly, within earshot of Smith, 'in the second half I'll play the ball inside the full-back to "The Gay" for him to run on to.' Gilzean hoped that Smith would complain about having to run for the ball instead of getting it to feet. Shankly snapped back: 'Christ Gillie, there's no need to get "effin" complicated!' A ball inside the full-back was complicated for Shankly. He preferred his players to go out and play what came naturally to them.

Bob Shankly, himself, had a sharp, if somewhat dry sense of humour and any time he heard a player being a little too big for his boots, he was able to knock him back down to size with a sharp retort. He also, however, always had praise and a kind word for his players in equal abundance when needed. Craig Brown recalls that Shankly often employed his sense of humour with the press. If he was keeping his team selection close to his chest he would tell them 'Oor Gretna (his wife) hasn't picked the team yet!'

Gilzean compares Shankly as similar in style to his manager at his next club, Tottenham: 'Shankly and Bill Nicholson were both hard workers, extremely honest and hard when they needed to be. Both had a drive to win things and do it if possible while playing flair football.' Gilzean finds it interesting that neither Shankly nor Nicholson were particularly skilful players themselves.

The week after recovering to beat Raith, Dundee were due at Hibs, Gordon Smith's first senior club. Having won three league medals as part of their Famous Five forward line, Smith was keen to impress. Impress he did, for he was instrumental in leading Dundee to a 3-1 win. To top it all, Gordon scored the third direct from a corner. For Dundee, not having won against either Hibs or Hearts in the capital for three years, it was a key victory. The result maintained Dundee's six-point advantage over Rangers, who scraped home 3-2 at Tannadice.

At the start of the season, the official Dundee Supporters Club showed a paltry membership of only 30 members. By late November that number had increased tenfold to 300. With numbers rapidly rising, thanks to the success on the park, the Supporters Club was now able to run its first bus to an away game – at Hibs – and also planned a social evening in Dundee's Whitehall Theatre, then primarily a cinema. The entertainment would include the popular Scottish traditional singers, The Alexander Brothers, who appeared on television in 'The Lucky White Heather Club', and also the newly formed Cortina Group, who were to be the Dundee Supporters Club resident band.

In 2001, the Dundee Supporters Association would also hold a concert in the city's Whitehall Theatre, following a similar increase in its membership, which again reflected better performances on the pitch. The club's unofficial band, 'Jump The Q', entertained with vastly different music to the traditional Scottish offering by The Cortina Band. Jump the Q's set included songs they had penned themselves, such as 'Dinna Bring An Arab Hame Tae Me', 'Cheer Up Alex Smith', and 'Dee Till Eh Deh'.

Chic McDonald, who lived in Isla Street off Dens Road, close to the ground, attended both concerts and remembers them as coming at a time when the profile of Dundee was being raised and folk were becoming more interested in the club. 'People in the city were becoming proud again to be a Dundee fan,' and the concerts gave Dundee supporters the opportunity to socialise and show their support for the club away from the ground.

One reason Bobby Wishart gives for the increase in Dundee's profile was the signing of Gordon Smith, which raised the media's interest in the club. 'Despite being fairly shy himself, Smith's success in his career so far meant that he was the only real glamorous player at the club, and the likes of Rex Kingsley of the *Sunday Mail* and Harry Andrews of the *Sunday Express* started coming to Dens more regularly. Gordon made a huge contribution to Dundee in this respect because once these writers came to Dens and saw the potential of the Dundee side start to unfold, they started to come back regularly and raise the profile of the club and of the emerging stars like Gilzean and Ure.'

Another group starting to take notice of Dundee's rise were the Scottish international selectors, who in November for the first time that century picked three Dundee players to play in the same Scottish team. The players in question were Alex Hamilton and Ian Ure – winning their fourth and second caps respectively – and Hugh Robertson, coming in for his first and only full international cap.

Helped no doubt by the club's climb to the top and by the recent 5-1 win at Ibrox, the Dundee trio were chosen to play against Czechoslovakia in Brussels in a World Cup play-off in a bid to qualify for the 1962 finals in Chile.

For Dundee to have three players in the Scottish side was a tremendous achievement. Ian Ure, whom many believe should have won more than his eleven international caps, was far from enamoured at the way the Scotland side was often picked. He remembers, for example, playing for Scotland when they beat Spain 6-2 in Real Madrid's Bernabau Stadium in 1963, but in the next match several players, including Ure, were replaced by others who had missed the Spanish game through injury. Ure himself spent most of his international career playing second fiddle to Celtic's Billy McNeill.

George Hamilton of Third Lanark remembers Hugh Robertson in particular being unlucky in only making one appearance for his country. He remembers Robertson as being a 'courageous little bundle of energy who was never beaten and who was never given a proper chance to recreate his club form at international level. He suffered from the fact that there were so many good wingers in Scotland at the time and the likes of Willie Henderson of Rangers and Jimmy Johnstone of Celtic, who both emerged shortly afterwards, would regularly fill the wide roles.'

'Shug' Robertson was signed for Dundee by Willie Thornton in 1957 from junior side Auchinleck Talbot and made his first-team debut the same year at the age of eighteen. He was originally a coal miner in his native Ayrshire before turning to full-time soccer and went on to make 276 appearances for the Dark Blues.

Shug stood 5ft 9in tall with short dark hair parted on the left side. He was a tricky ball player with an elusive style whose crosses were well placed and flighted. Gilzean remembers Shug as 'a little terrier who had lots of skill, was very tricky and could turn on a sixpence'. Bobby Wishart adds that the Dundee side were extremely skilful but not particularly pacy, and the wide players like Smith and Robertson used skill rather than speed to beat their opponents.

Wishart also put Robertson into a group of players whose contribution to Dundee's success was often overlooked because of the stars elsewhere in the team. Wishart says: 'no matter what the likes of Robertson, Cousin or Seith would do, the press on a Sunday would always pick the same star players of Smith, Gilzean or Ure, but the contributions of those players and other should never be underestimated.'

In the first week of December, Dundee's winning league sequence of ten games would surely not be threatened by the visit of bottom-placed Stirling Albion. But it was. The game ended 2-2, and although it represented an unexpected point dropped, Dundee were relieved by the end to have come away with anything. They had been behind at the break and had seen Stirling have two goals chopped off late on.

The conditions were treacherous – wet, windy and icy – and at the finish the tannoy announcer appealed to spectators to take their time leaving the stadium and be careful on the terracing and stairs. Just 11,500 hardy souls had braved the Arctic conditions for Dundee's lowest home gate of the season but, curiously, the attendance was identical to that for the next home game, against Airdrie, on 16 December.

The players were keen to make amends for the disappointing performance against Albion by turning it on against the team just one place higher. This time the form-book prevailed and Dundee produced the goods in a 5-1 win to record their highest home victory of the season.

Bob Shankly, however, was more concerned about the second poor attendance in a row. In his post-match interviews he concentrated not on the excellent win but on delivering an appeal to the Dundee fans to come out and watch his side:

'I am very disappointed in the recent crowds at Dens and I urge the Dundee public to come out now and support my team,' Shankly said in the *Sporting Post* that night. 'We have a great chance to create some history here and my team deserve more support than we are getting. What do the Dundee supporters want for them to come out and support us? We haven't lost in almost four months, are top of the league, and have played some good football along the way. We have proven that we can beat both Rangers and Celtic and if we are going to go on and achieve success this year we need all Dundee fans to come out and cheer the team to victory.'

Shankly hardly got his wish the following week, when barely 100 supporters followed the team to St Mirren but, with it being 23 December, the crowds on the Saturday before Christmas are traditionally the poorest attended matches of the season.

There was more discontent for Shankly, however, as top goalscorer Gilzean failed for the second match in a row to be fit. As in the Airdrie game, he was replaced by George McGeachie, who would play at outside-right, with Gordon Smith moving into Gilzean's more central position.

Gilzean had unknowingly fractured his jaw in the draw with Stirling Albion. He had not been missed against Airdrie but now, against the Buddies, his scoring prowess was missed. Dundee failed to sparkle and were held to their second draw in three games.

Taking charge of the Saints for his first match was former Dundee favourite Bobby Flavell, who had replaced Willie Reid in the Paisley hot seat. Flavell had played in the successful Dundee side of the early 1950s with Billy Steel and won two League Cup winners medals with the Dees. Flavell had been Dundee's top scorer in both those seasons but all he was interested in now was denting Dundee's championship challenge. In fact, the draw extended Dundee's lead at the top to six points, as Rangers surprisingly crashed 2-4 at Ibrox to Aberdeen.

The following week, on 30 December, Dundee's home fixture against St Johnstone was postponed due to a snow-covered pitch, but the enforced break at least gave Gilzean another week to recover from his broken jaw. This allowed him to reclaim his place at the expense of the unlucky McGeachie for the visit of Falkirk on 6 January. The match was fortunate to go ahead as the Dens pitch was still covered by a hard frost.

Gilzean, however, came up with an inventive way to combat the hard surface. Instead of lining up in football boots, he took the field in sand-shoes, in the hope that they would stop him losing his footing on the slippy surface. His ingenuity was rewarded as Gillie notched both Dundee goals in a 2-1 win. Partick Thistle had now sneaked into second place, five points behind Dundee, with Celtic sitting a further point back in third. But Dundee were under no illusions about the threat posed by fourth-placed Rangers.

	P	W	D	L	F	A	Pts
Dundee	17	14	2	1	52	20	30
Partick	19	12	1	6	40	32	25
Celtic	18	10	4	4	47	22	24
Rangers	17	10	3	4	40	20	24

At the halfway point of the season, Dundee had accumulated 30 points. Another 30 in the second half would see them home and dry. Rangers now won a rearranged game against Hearts 2-1 in midweek. The following Saturday Hearts faced Dundee at Tynecastle, and Hearts manager Tommy Walker made an astonishing seven changes from his side which had lost in Govan.

Dundee took a risk with Gordon Smith, who had been badly shaken in a car crash. He had been involved in a collision on the road from his home in North Berwick to Edinburgh and was lucky to come off no worse. Smith was determined to play against his former club and told Shankly as much when he met up with his team-mates in Gorgie.

Despite sitting mid-table, Hearts had had a decent campaign to date. They had reached the League Cup final, losing to Rangers in a replay, and been beaten 0-1 by Inter Milan at Tynecastle in the Inter-Cities Fairs Cup. The gamble over Smith paid off, however, as Gordon was involved in both Dundee goals, setting up Cousin and Gilzean.

In their next two matches, Dundee faced two of the three sides to have beaten them so far – Aberdeen (in the league) and Third Lanark (in the League Cup). The Aberdeen match in particular gave Dundee the chance to put the record straight.

During the build up, the Dundee players insisted this was the chance for payback against Aberdeen. To add extra spice, the referee, Mr A Crossman from Edinburgh, was the villain who had officiated at Pittodrie and awarded the Dons a cruel, match-turning penalty.

Alex Hamilton in particular was looking for revenge, because it was against him that the penalty was conceded. In the *Evening Telegraph* the day before the Wednesday evening match, Hamilton noted: 'We are really fired up for tomorrow's game and are looking to get revenge for our only league defeat of the season. We felt hard done by up there as it was never a penalty in the first match. I cleanly headed it away and we won't need any more motivation when we take the field than to remember the disappointment on the journey home.'

Hamilton and Dundee got their revenge all right as they won the match 2-1. In one of football's many ironies, the winning goal came from a controversial penalty given this time in Dundee's favour. Referee Crossman awarded the spot-kick to Dundee when he adjudged Dons full-back Bennett to have handled a Hugh Robertson cross. Aberdeen protested vehemently and manager Tommy Pearson made his feelings known to the linesman, but the award stood and 'Penalty King' Penman notched his fifth spot-kick for the Dees.

Aberdeen fan Tommy Beattie remembers the Dundee championship side well and recalls some similarities with the Aberdeen side which won the league title in 1955. Tam recalls that the Dons side of seven years earlier had a core of three young players – Leggat, Caldwell and Bobby Wishart – and three older, experienced players in Mitchell, Buckley and Alex Young. He notes that the Dundee side in 1962 had exactly the same blend. For Dundee, the older players were Seith, Smith and the same Bobby Wishart, while the younger jewels were Ure, Penman and Alan Gilzean.

Having struck the penalty winner against Aberdeen, Penman showed off his prowess from the spot again three days later when he opened the scoring in a 2-1 home win over Third Lanark. Mid-table Thirds had conceded only 28 goals to date, just one more than leaders Dundee, so beating a side which had twice troubled them in the League Cup was a potential banana skin avoided.

In winning the championship, Dundee conceded a surprisingly large number of goals for title-winners – 46, compared to 31 by second-placed Rangers and 37 by third-placed Celtic. This is, however, in no way a slight on the Dundee rearguard, whose quality was appreciated by everyone. According to Bobby Wishart, the high goals-against figure was more a reflection of the attacking nature of the team. That season saw a number of high-scoring matches which Dundee won, namely 5-3 over Killie, and 5-4 and 3-2 over Raith. This allowed Dundee to win the title while conceding only seven goals fewer than in the preceding season, when they had finished tenth.

On 20 January 1962 Dundee established a club record which still stands today – twenty games undefeated That milestone was reached when they defeated St Johnstone 2-1 in a rearranged home fixture. Since losing at Pittodrie in September, Dundee had gone eighteen league games undefeated, won a friendly against Swedish champions Elfsborg Boras, and won the Dewar Shield when they overcame St Johnstone back in October.

The Dewar Shield was competed for annually by the winners of the Forfarshire, Aberdeenshire, Perthshire, and Stirlingshire Cups. Victory over St Johnstone had constituted the final of the previous, 1960-61 tournament, after Dundee had won the 1959-60 Forfarshire Cup. Dundee had been unable to squeeze in that final in the 1960-61 season, so it was held over until the following year.

Regional cup competitions were still considered fairly important in the Scottish football calendar in 1962, but the advent of European football meant that they assumed a progressively lower profile throughout the 1960s and '70s. Today, many clubs enter their youth teams into local cup competitions. Dundee, as traditional members of the Forfarshire Football Association, now compete in the tournament with their under-21 side. The Dewar Shield itself is now defunct. Dundee last contested it in 1976 when they belatedly completed the 1972 tournament by beating Keith 6-0 in front of 600 fans. In 1961, Dundee fielded a full-strength side which defeated St Johnstone 4-2 at Dens before 3,000 spectators.

Dundee's impressive unbeaten run came to a crushing end in the most important cup competition of all, the Scottish Cup. Dundee had been lucky to get a bye in the first round, back in December, and now in the second round they had been drawn at home to St Mirren, with whom they had recently drawn 1-1 in the league in Paisley.

As league leaders and unbeaten for five months, Dundee were overwhelming favourites, but according to Norrie Price in *Up Wi' The Bonnets,* 'in recent games Dundee had lived dangerously and there were signs that the strain was beginning to tell. Some fans were heard to voice concern at how their favourites could possibly cope with a cup run on top of their point-gathering exertions.'

Ian Ure, however, was looking forward to the Cup as 'it was in many ways the competition to win as cup finals and internationals were the glamorous matches that every player wanted to play in, compared to the bread and butter of the league'.

In the event, Dundee were undone by a hungrier St Mirren side who won the tie 1-0 in front of 22,000 Dens spectators. St Mirren, who would go on to reach the final, had taken a relaxed approach in the build up.

They had gone for a stroll on Broughty Ferry beach on the morning of the game, having arrived by train from Paisley, and it paid off as the Buddies pulled off one of the surprises of the round. The winning goal was scored by inside-forward George McLean, whom Bobby Wishart remembers as a big, lanky, tricky player who often scored important goals and always caused Dundee problems.

Concerns over how Dundee might handle simultaneous league and cup runs had vanished even before they had begun. Even though the team were now free to concentrate on the league, the Cup defeat actually signalled the start of a dreadful slump. The following week, away to Kilmarnock, Shankly expressed confidence in the team who had crashed to the Buddies. But it took Cousin's late strike to rescue a point that was barely deserved.

With Rangers winning 4-0 at home to Airdrie, Dundee's lead was cut to five points. The gap was closed even more seven days later when Dundee crashed to their first home league defeat of the season.

Against Kilmarnock, Craig Brown had made his Dundee debut when he replaced skipper Bobby Cox, out with an injured knee, and against Motherwell, Brown retained his place with Cox having failed to make a recovery.

Motherwell, considered by Bob Crampsey to be one of the best sides in Scotland at the time, dished out Dundee's first home defeat, and as the Dark Blues had led 1-0 at half-time, the alarm bells started to ring when they conceded three second-half goals.

Dundee took a welcome break the following week, heading down to London to face Arsenal at Highbury in a friendly. Both clubs had been knocked out of their respective Cups. Arsenal would head north in March for a second friendly after hosting Dundee on 17 February. Despite recent setbacks, Dundee acquitted themselves pretty well at Highbury. The *Courier* reported that 'on paper the result was 2-2 but there was no doubt of the superiority of Dundee. Londoners believe that football begins and ends north of the Thames with the so successful Spurs and the not-so-successful Arsenal. Dundee however shook the 16,340 fans at Highbury with a display that says a lot for the standard of Scottish football.'

Dundee lined up: Liney, Hamilton, Brown, Seith, Ure, Wishart, Smith, Cousin, Waddell, Gilzean, Robertson – with Seith taking over as captain again in Cox's absence. Arsenal's team was: Kelsey, Bacuzzi, McCullough, Sneddon, Neill, Clamp, Skirton, Barnwell, Brown, Eastham, McLeod.

Dundee's fragile confidence was shattered again when league business resumed on 24 February. The team crashed to their biggest defeat of the season, 0-3 at Partick Thistle. The result allowed Rangers to pull to within one point of Dundee as the league title race was blown wide open.

	P	W	D	L	F	A	Pts
Dundee	24	18	3	3	62	30	39
Rangers	24	17	4	3	65	24	38
Celtic	25	14	6	5	64	31	34
Hearts	26	14	5	7	47	37	33

According to Dundee FC historian Norrie Price, 'too many of the players had started to believe in the team's invincibility and as their attitude slackened, the tide had turned in the other direction.'

After the promising display against Arsenal, it was puzzling as to why Dundee should struggle when they returned to Scotland. In London, however, the Highbury playing surface had been excellent for the time of year, and may well have suited Dundee's style of play compared to the heavy pitches in Scotland.

This was borne out by Ian Ure, when assessing Dundee's slump. He explained to Jim Hendry in *Dundee Greats*: 'There is no doubt in my mind that the good grounds in the early part of the season suited our game to perfection. We definitely started to believe we were top notchers and the feeling about was that we would only have to coast through the rest of the season. Unfortunately, all these wee things got to us psychologically – you try that wee half ounce less and before you know what's happening, things are slipping.'

Away from football, March 1962 saw Dundee's first Ten-Pin bowling alley opened in the basement of The Golden Pheasant pub in Downfield. While white skittles were starting to be knocked down, Dundee's title hopes looked to be going the same way. Rangers went top of the league for the first time since September when they defeated Motherwell in a rearranged game on 28 February and, despite having played a game more, it was a severe blow to the Dees.

On 3 March, Dundee travelled to Celtic Park, looking to end their poor run. It was hoped that the return of skipper Bobby Cox would inspire the Dark Blues back to winning ways. Cox had recovered from his knee trouble and urged his team-mates 'to recover their fight'. It was going to be tough against a Celtic side undefeated at home all season, which had lost only once in their last eighteen games, and who had not given up hope of winning the league themselves.

Shankly made three changes to his team in the hope of freshening things up. Cox returned, Penman was dropped, Wishart moved to inside-right, and Craig Brown from left-back to wing-half. It would be Wishart's first Dundee appearance at inside-right. For Celtic, future Lisbon Lion Bobby Lennox made his debut.

Despite an improved performance, Dundee still went down 1-2. Celtic recovered from Wishart's second-half opener to win the game with two late strikes. With Smith hirpling with a thigh injury, Celtic capitalised in front of the biggest league crowd Dundee would play in front of all season. The winner came from Celtic's captain, Billy McNeill, who impressed the watching Scottish League selectors sufficiently to oust Ian Ure from the Scottish League side to face England the following Friday. Ure reckoned, however, that his fate had been already sealed by his poor performance at Partick the week before.

With Rangers having beaten Third Lanark 3-1, Dundee had fallen three points behind their rivals, but they had a quick opportunity to close the gap when they played their game in hand against Dunfermline the following Wednesday.

Gordon Smith failed to recover from an injury picked up at Parkhead, so Andy Penman returned for the visit of the Pars. Without Smith's guile and flair, Dundee failed to present any attacking threat and lost (1-2) for the fourth game in a row.

	P	W	D	L	F	A	Pts
Rangers	26	19	4	3	70	25	42
Dundee	26	18	3	5	64	40	39
Celtic	26	15	6	5	66	32	36

The return friendly against Arsenal on Saturday, 10 March brought little respite for the Dark Blues, who lost 0-1. Dundee lined up with Liney, Hamilton, Cox, Seith, Ure, Brown, Penman, Gilzean, Waddell, Cousin and Robertson. They did not call upon Gordon Smith, who had captained Hibs against Arsenal back in 1952, when Hibs lost 1-7. Arsenal's eleven was: Kelsey, Bacuzzi, McCullough, Clamp, Brown, Groves, Clapton, Barnwell, Strong, Eastham, and Skirton.

Arsenal brought with them one supporter, 19-year-old Fred Renvoize from Longfield Avenue, Middlesex, who had travelled up overnight from London on the train. Fred had not missed an Arsenal away fixture for five years and was keen to keep his proud record going with his visit to Dens Park. He became quite a character on matchday as he mixed with the Dundee supporters on the terracing. Wearing a red and white bonnet which had picture badges of every Arsenal player, he regaled listeners with stories of Arsenal and their history to everyone within earshot before and after the match, at half-time and whenever there was a lull in the game.

For Dundee, the match solved none of their problems. Bob Shankly tried an experimental forward line and Arsenal played at a speed that Dundee were unable to match. Arsenal's goal was scored by £50,000 forward George Eastham, whose smooth, silky touches delighted the 10,000 crowd, many of whom, dismayed by Dundee's seven-week winless run, scurried away home long before the match was finished.

The advantage had been well and truly handed to the reigning champions, Rangers. Dundee's alarming winter slump had seen them squander an eight-point lead. According to Ure, the press had Dundee believing after Christmas that the league was 'a one horse race, a cakewalk for Dundee', but their winter of discontent had now left Rangers romping away at the top.

With Rangers next to visit Dens, many doubted Dundee's ability to recover the lost ground as the dreams of a first elusive championship seemed to be slipping inexorably away.

Chapter 5

~ Fight To The Finish ~

(March 1962 – April 1962)

In just five short weeks, Dundee had gone from 'cock-of-the-walk' league leaders, eight points clear of Rangers, to potential 'also-rans', three points behind the men from Govan after a shattering loss of form. After riding high, twenty games undefeated, Dundee came crashing back to earth, out of the Scottish Cup, and seemingly out of contention for the League. Their last chance of rescuing their season arrived on Wednesday, 14 March, when Rangers came to Dens.

That morning the Dundee *Courier* noted that the match 'could be the most fateful night in the history of Dundee FC'. A defeat would leave Dundee virtual spectators in the title race, but a win would cut Rangers' lead to one point, with seven games remaining.

Dundee fans were also wondering what team Shankly would send out. Who will be in? and who will be out? The letters pages in the local press had been dominated for weeks by that question. Shankly had two massive choices to make. Gilzean was down with flu and Gordon Smith still struggling with the leg injury which had forced him to sit out the defeat by Dunfermline. During the Tuesday press conference Shankly gave a broad hint of his thinking: 'We must win tomorrow night and I can't afford to gamble on a youngster hitting it off. The result means too much for that. It is not a question of lack of ability in the side at all, as we've proved we have that, but the side is just not clicking. The big occasion may put the boys back on the rails.'

Perhaps Bob Shankly was trying to throw his opposite number, Scot Symon, off the scent. Either way, he had no choice but to field one of his youngsters, Bobby Waddell, for Gilzean, still bedridden with flu. There was better news on Gordon Smith, who reclaimed his place. In the three days leading up to the game he had been the first to arrive at Dens in the morning, despite having to get up in his North Berwick home at 5.30am. He took part in a practice match on the Tuesday and declared to Tommy Gallacher of the *Courier* that his leg had made a full recovery: 'You can't rule me out for tomorrow now.'

Shankly held a team conference with his players on the Tuesday afternoon, following a full-scale practice match. Alan Cousin remembers that he gave his squad a huge vote of confidence. 'Shanks told us although we had gone through a bad spell, he had faith in us and that he wanted us to go out the following night and justify it.'

Rangers had their own selection problems. Right-back Bobby Shearer turned up at Ibrox on Monday with sore ribs and was promptly sent for an X-ray to check for a suspected break. Another problem for Scot Symon was that Jim Baxter was due to play for the Army versus the Navy in Aldershot that same night. Just 24 hours before kick-off, Symon was still awaiting the outcome of an appeal, requesting Baxter's release. Baxter's regular stand in, Billy Stevenson, was also an injury doubt.

Shearer's X-ray showed bruised ribs, no break, but his chances were still rated as only 50-50. Shearer had played 63 consecutive games for his club and the last Rangers match he had missed had been against Dundee, on 8 February the previous year. Determined not to break this sequence, Shearer declared himself fit. Less happily for Symon, the appeal for Baxter's release was unsuccessful. The Army had been slow to reply to Rangers' request, so 'Slim Jim' had been forced to leave his Cowdenbeath home at mid-day Tuesday and take the train to London in case the appeal failed. Once he was travelling, the Army saw little point in agreeing to Rangers' request, and Symon felt the club had been stitched up.

Despite it being a Wednesday evening, the 35,000 crowd was Dens' biggest gate of the season and the biggest at home since 42,500 watched a Scottish Cup-tie against Rangers in 1956. One fan determined not to miss out was Dundee-born Neil Kirk, who lived in New York. Kirk had come over and seen both of Rangers' League Cup-ties in August, but not the classic 5-1 win at Ibrox in November. He now rearranged a business trip to iron out the details of a ten-week tour of America for Scots comic Jimmy Logan and other artistes, taking in the Dens match.

Kirk had in fact arrived on the Saturday before, to see the game when it was originally scheduled, but when he touched down at Prestwick Airport he was told it had been postponed due to Rangers having to play Kilmarnock in the quarter-final of the Scottish Cup. Undaunted, he took in the Cup-tie at Rugby Park and thought Rangers 'no great shakes'. Now, like thousands of home-based Dundonians, he was hoping that he would not have to revise his assessment.

Bobby Wishart again missed out, and was replaced by Craig Brown at left-half. Jim Baxter's stand in was Billy Stevenson. The Rangers team had one thing on their minds – revenge for the 5-1 Ibrox massacre. To do that they had to extend Dundee's losing sequence to five.

The only winner was the tension, for the contest drifted to a disappointing 0-0 stalemate. It was Dundee's seventh game without a win but at least it stopped the rot and prevented the Gers pulling five points clear. In terms of the championship, it was still 'game on'. According to Bobby Cox, Dundee's gritty performance 'restored a lot of the confidence that had been missing in recent games'. The *Daily Record* claimed: 'it was a match which Dundee should have won … Dundee showed the spirit, power and skill of heroes.'

	P	W	D	L	F	A	Pts
Rangers	27	19	5	3	70	25	43
Dundee	27	18	4	5	64	40	40
Celtic	26	15	6	5	66	32	36

It was now vital for Dundee to pick up momentum. Being three points behind Rangers, there could be no further slip-ups. Three days later the Dees travelled to face Raith Rovers, who were just one place above the drop zone. Like Rangers, Raith were also out for revenge, in their case to put right their 5-4 defeat, when Dundee fought back from 2-4 down with a winner in injury-time.

The Dundee players travelled by train, having to cross into Fife on the Tay Rail Bridge. On board, the players mixed with fans who were journeying to the game. Dundee supporter Graham McKay remembers: 'One of my highlights as a Dundee fan came for me in the championship season when I met the players coming off the same train at Kirkcaldy before we played Raith in March. We hadn't won a game for two months yet the players seemed extremely confident. They were not only going to win that day but were going to go on and win the league. Alex Hamilton told me, my dad, and a group of other Dundee fans who had come off the train, that we were going to catch Rangers and win the league and we believed him. He was so enthusiastic but he was right. We did, but for a while it hadn't looked too good.'

Prior to the Rangers game, keeper Pat Liney had been presented with a good luck charm from Dundee supporters who, like Graham McKay, feared that the slump may cost Dundee the league. In 1990, Liney shared memories of the title win in a birthday letter to supporter Jim Mitchell: 'During the season when we hit a bad spell, a lady and her daughter presented me with a lucky charm. It was a little seal carved from wood and covered with skin from a seal in the Tay. It had the team colours in a ribbon around the neck. I am not a superstitious person but the little girl said that it always brought her luck and we never lost a game after that. I still have the seal and maybe I should send it to Gordon Wallace for next season.' (It might have been a good idea to send it to Wallace, Dundee's manager at the time, but Liney obviously never did, as Dundee were relegated under Wallace in 1990 and failed to get promotion in 1991.)

Having put a brake on the slump against Rangers after Liney accepted the wooden seal, Dundee returned to winning ways at Kirkcaldy. Despite twice going behind, Dundee bounced back to win 3-2. Their unusual tactics of bombarding Rovers in the air paid off, despite the absence of aerial master Gilzean. ('Gilzean had such a great spring that would allow him to leap high above any defender,' Dundee historian Norrie Price often muses.) The Dees were also lucky to survive two first-half penalty appeals, when the ball twice hit Ure's arm. Reprieved, Dundee pumped crosses into the Raith defenders, where Shankly had spotted a weakness. Robertson and Smith played crosses in at the earliest opportunity and Penman headed home a brace to allow Dundee to earn the two points for the first time since 24 January.

Rangers, however, retained their three-point lead after a 7-1 blitz at Falkirk, but the following week the pendulum started to swing Dundee's way, when they got some help from an unexpected source. At a wet and windy Dens Park, Dundee beat Hibs 1-0, courtesy of a goal from Gilzean's understudy, Bobby Waddell. Rangers, meanwhile, lost 0-1 at Ibrox to Dundee United. Wishart remembers: 'We couldn't believe our luck when we heard that United had won at Ibrox as it allowed us to make up some vital ground that we hadn't expected. It gave us the belief that the championship could still be won, as Rangers weren't infallible and could drop points.'

Bobby Cox was even more positive when talking to the *Courier*: 'If we win every game until the end of the season, there is nothing Rangers can do about it [Dundee winning their games] and I feel we can win the league.' Most Dundee fans weren't so sure, as the post-bags in both local papers, the *Courier* and the *Evening Telegraph*, revealed. While American President Kennedy was arguing with Kruschev about nuclear testing, Dundee fans were arguing about the best team selections and were, on the whole, still negative about the Dark Blues' chances. The *Courier* exasperatedly described the Dundee fans as 'fickle'.

The following week Dundee reclaimed top spot, as Rangers were otherwise engaged in a Scottish Cup semi-final against Motherwell. Dundee made heavy weather of beating bottom club Stirling Albion 3-2, but it was enough to put Dundee back on top by one point.

	P	W	D	L	F	A	Pts
Dundee	30	21	4	5	71	44	46
Rangers	29	20	5	4	77	27	45

Gilzean's return at Annfield was a boost, and he capped his return by scoring the winning goal after Stirling had twice equalised. Before going down with influenza, Gilzean had represented Scotland Under-23s against England at Pittodrie, where he lined up against his future strike partner at Tottenham, Jimmy Greaves. England won 4-2. Gillie scored one and Greaves two, but it was the chirpy Cockney whom the sports pages raved about the next day.

Speaking many years later, Gilzean recalled his playing days: 'Jimmy was fantastic to play with. I was fortunate to strike up a good partnership with Greavesie and he was the best finisher I ever saw. He had half a second more than anyone else and could dribble at speed as well as finish. My partnership with Jimmy was different to the one I had at Dens with Alan Cousin, as Alan did a tremendous amount of work, grafting and laying off balls while I did the scoring, while at Spurs my role was reversed as I did the hard work for Jimmy to do all the scoring. I was very lucky to have Alan at Dens and Jimmy at White Hart Lane.'

Gilzean's return was crucial to Dundee, as he notched five goals in the final five games, but one man who missed out was Craig Brown, who never featured again after damaging his left knee against Stirling. Brown had done well after coming in, first for Cox, then for Wishart, and the *Courier* described him as 'a definite success during Dundee's lean period'. In his autobiography Brown makes light of the fact that his run in the side coincided with Dundee's losing spell, but in truth he had let no one down and was even nominated Dundee's man of the match following the defeat at Parkhead in March. The frustrated Brown now had to spend his time recuperating in Dundee's Fernbrae Nursing Home, and was forced to scramble for news of his team-mates in newspapers, on radio and on television.

Dundee next faced Airdrie on 7 April, by which time Rangers had been restored to the top after beating St Johnstone in midweek. Dundee's line up was back to its recognisable first-choice eleven, with Wishart replacing Brown. In fact, the team would be unchanged for the rest of the season. Airdrie were fighting for their lives in the relegation zone. They cancelled out Penman's goal on the stroke of half-time, but were beaten in controversial circumstances. When Cousin's shot was punched over the crossbar by Airdrie left-back Shanks, referee Wilkie at first awarded a corner, but was surrounded by furious Dundee players. The referee agreed to consult his linesman and, to Dundee's relief, changed his mind and awarded a spot-kick to the Dees. Penman scored, but with Rangers winning 1-0 at Ibrox against Dunfermline, the status quo was maintained.

Easter Monday, two days later, was when derby games were traditionally scheduled. With three games left and one point separating the top two, Rangers were at Parkhead while Dundee were at Tannadice. Bob Shankly's daughter had recently become engaged to United left-back Jimmy Briggs, but Briggs was in no mood to do any favours for his future father-in-law. He was in the newspaper Monday morning stating how determined United were to win the match.

It is perhaps surprising to hear that in 1962 many United supporters would not have begrudged Dundee winning the championship. United fan Gordon King, for example, was performing his National Service in Germany at the time. Looking back, Gordon felt that 'despite the rivalry between the clubs, Dundee's league win was good for the city'. Dundee United's current programme editor, Peter Rundo, recalls that he was one of only two United fans in his school class at Harris Academy (the other was Ally Dailly, father of Christian), and he wasn't put out by Dundee's title success.

Peter is puzzled by the contrary reaction from Dundee fans when United won the Premier League in 1983. But a lot had passed between the clubs in the intervening twenty-odd years. I was the same age when United won the Scottish title as Peter was when Dundee won it, but our feelings at the time were in complete contrast. I was at Dens Park the day the Arabs beat us 2-1 to win the league and I could not bear the thought of them being crowned champions. I had grown up to see Dundee relegated on goal-difference in the first season of the new Premier League while United had stayed up after finishing level on points with Dundee. United fans revelled in their new status as top club in the city and United rubbed salt in our wounds by winning their first ever trophy at Dens when they beat Aberdeen in a League Cup final replay in 1979. United then retained the trophy, this time beating us in the final at Dens, and then handed out to Dundee the ultimate insult when they won the league at Dens.

United, in other words, claimed their first three trophies at the home of their nearest rivals, two of them by beating Dundee. In contrast to Peter, I was one of only three Dundee supporters in my class at Rockwell Primary. The Monday after United won the league, school was a nightmare. The first thing I saw was a United fan sporting a huge badge on his blazer. It read: 'We won the league at Dens – Fly the Flag.' It hurt.

Dundee went into the final derby of 1961-62 knowing that they were in for a tough game. Craig Brown recalls that after doing Dundee a favour by winning at Ibrox, 'United were no less determined to beat us in the return local derby game in April.'

Bob Miller's report in the *People's Journal* after Dundee had beaten Stirling on 31 March stated 'Dundee should hammer the lot – except maybe United.' United were clearly going to have a big say in the destiny of the flag. The press build up was intense, with the *Evening Telegraph* running a special early edition which would include a half-time report.

Dundee supporter Derek Burgess remembers a cup-tie atmosphere at Tannadice which was full to the rafters with a 20,000 all-ticket crowd. The match lived up to expectations. United took the lead through Jim Irvine, but Gilzean pulled the sides level before the break. There was just four minutes to go when Gilzean thundered a 25-yarder into the top corner of the United goal.

Derek reflects, 'I can still see Gillie's late winner, a powerful shot which flew past Ugolini, as if it was yesterday.' Gilzean remembers the game well and says that 'the first was definitely thanks to United keeper Ronald Ugolini, as my speculative shot bounced as it approached the goal and he dived over the top of it. The second, from about 25 yards out, screamed right into the top corner and the win was crucial in a very difficult game. It was a huge step for us.'

The news that greeted the Dundee players in the dressing room was that Rangers had been held 1-1 at Celtic. Dundee and Rangers were now level on points, but Rangers were still top on goal average.

	P	W	D	L	F	A	Pts
Rangers	32	22	6	4	83	29	50
Dundee	32	23	4	6	75	46	50

Both clubs now had to wait a couple of weeks to resume their championship duel. In the interim, Scotland took on England at Hampden, and that was followed by the Scottish Cup final between Rangers and St Mirren. Although the league was not scheduled to be interrupted, both Rangers and Dundee had players in the Scottish side, and so postponed their respective fixtures. Dundee's match against St Mirren would have gone ahead, except that the Paisley club had a date at Hampden. In short, the race for the championship would not resume until Wednesday, 25 April.

On Saturday, 14 April, Alex Hamilton was in the Scotland side which ended their 25-year Hampden hoodoo with a 2-0 win over England. For Hamilton, known around Dens Park as 'Hammy', that was his fourth full cap. He would go on, after being described in 1962 by the *Daily Record* as 'the international find of the season', to become the most capped player in Dundee's history with 24 caps.

Hailing from Fauldhouse in West Lothian, Hamilton signed for Dundee in 1957 from juvenile side Westrigg Bluebell, despite missing a penalty when the then manager, Willie Thornton, was watching. Hamilton had been working as an insurance agent at the behest of his mother, but he was destined for great things in the dark blue of Dundee and Scotland. Hammy didn't have to wait long for his first-team debut. He started in a 2-4 defeat at Hearts in the League Cup on 31 August 1957. By the end of that season, the right-back had made 21 appearances, and in a total of eleven years with Dundee he would make 338 appearances for the club in all competitions.

Hamilton was a favourite with the fans and popular in the dressing room, and his team-mates talk about him with fondness. Hammy was instantly recognisable with his snappy fair-haired crew-cut and a cheeky impish smile that was infectious to everyone around him.

At 5ft 7in, he wasn't the best defender in the air, but Hammy's skills lay in becoming one of the first overlapping full-backs in the Scottish game. With an abundance of pace, he is remembered by Ian Ure as 'a player who oozed talent and flair who was as lively a character as you'll ever meet'.

Bobby Wishart recalls that everyone at the club got on well together, which was part of its success, and describes Hamilton as 'a livewire, a joker and trickster'. He says that 'Hammy's gang of Robertson, Ure, and Gillie were always up to something' and that 'he always liked to wind up the other lads, especially Bobby Cox, about how many Scottish caps he had'. Gilzean adds: 'Hammy was a great character and an unbelievable guy,' and remembers that when the striker played in front of the south stand he, Gillie, would shout to the Dundee fans 'here comes the Hammy magic' and 'watch out for the Hammy magic'.

One time, however, this nearly backfired on Hammy, Gilzean recalls, when a fan in the terracing started to shout back at him. 'During the slump, when he lost a few games in a row, this supporter started to shout back to Hammy, "where's the effin magic now Hammy eh?" and gave him stick every time he went to take a throw in at that side. Hammy didn't like it very much and despite the fact that this guy was 6ft 5in or something, and a big bruiser, he [Hammy] shouted back, "meet me at the player's entrance afterwards and we'll sort it then."

'When we were getting changed in the dressing room afterwards, Hammy came over to me and said "Gillie, do me a favour and come out with me in case that guy's there. I doubt he will be but you never know, especially as we lost." Sure enough, when we got outside the big bruiser was there and Hammy, who couldn't fight for toffee, didn't know what to say. The bruiser said: "Hamilton, me and you Gussie Park now and we'll sort it." (Gussie Park was a bit of wasteland behind Dens and Tannadice which often housed carnivals and is now the site of Dundee United's all-weather astroturf training pitch). To get rid of the guy, Hammy told him he was only joking and had to give him a fiver to go and get himself a drink, and a fiver in those days would have got the lad a few drinks. Hammy thought he was invincible however!'

Hamilton lined up against England seven times in his career (three league caps and four full caps) and was never on a losing side. Hammy lined up opposite Bobby Charlton on a number of occasions and told Jim Hendry in *Dundee Greats* that, after one match at Hampden, a Scotland player shouted to Alf Ramsey, 'if you're looking for Bobby Charlton, you'd best check our hamper as he might still be in Hammy's back pocket!'

Hamilton's daughter, Sandi, met Bobby Charlton recently when she was a guest with her in-laws at Old Trafford. She was introduced to Sir Bobby as the daughter of one of his rivals from the 1960s. To give Charlton a clue to his identity, their host said to Charlton, 'in my pocket'. That was the only clue needed for Sir Bobby to instantly recognise Sandi as being Alex Hamilton's daughter.

No one who met Hamilton or saw him play will ever forget him. There is a hospitality lounge bearing his name at Dens today. Hammy and full-back partner Bobby Cox acted as hosts in the early 1990s in the Dens Park lounges and he had lost none of his sense of mischief. He entertained the guests hilariously, often employing Bobby Cox as an Ernie Wise to his Eric Morecambe!

The week after Hammy starred against England, Dundee were again inactive, as opponents St Mirren, having knocked Dundee out in the second round, contested the Scottish Cup final against Rangers. Rangers won 2-0 and, having claimed the League Cup earlier in the season, were now in pursuit of the 'treble'. The treble was, of course, a relatively new target, as the League Cup was a post-1945 innovation. But it had been achieved once, by Rangers, back in Dundee's disaster season, 1948-49. According to the *Rangers Historian*, in 1962 Rangers were now determined to win the championship to write themselves into the history books.

To do that they would have to overcome Aberdeen at Pittodrie and then Kilmarnock at Ibrox, while Dundee would have to beat St Mirren at Dens and St Johnstone away. With their vastly superior goal average, Rangers still were the obvious favourites.

The night of the St Mirren match is described by Jim Hendry as 'a night that no Dundee fan of that era could ever forget'.

St Mirren were desperate for points to avoid relegation and were eager to bounce back from the disappointment of losing the Scottish Cup final five days earlier. They had beaten Dundee at Dens in the Cup in January, and Dundee survived a George McLean header against a post before Alan Cousin fired in a low shot. At half-time the exciting news was that Aberdeen were leading Rangers 1-0 at Pittodrie.

Twelve minutes from time disaster struck when Gordon Smith handled in the box, and no amount of Dundee protests could prevent referee Willie Syme – who consulted his linesman – confirming the penalty. Journalist Bob Crampsey shared a car with Syme back to Glasgow after the match, and while Crampsey believed the decision to have been correct, he was curious why Syme had felt the need to check with his linesman. Syme's reply indicates the different codes under which the game was played then. He told Crampsey: 'I have refereed Mr [Gordon] Smith for fifteen years and in all that time I have never known him to query a decision.' The implication is that Gordon Smith was so honest that he would never protest against a decision unless he was confident it was wrong.

The penalty was taken by Paisley skipper Jim Clunie, who aimed towards the top right-hand corner, only to see Pat Liney twist in mid-air to claw the ball to safety. Almost immediately Dundee went up the park and scored the clincher through Andy Penman.

At the final whistle the Dundee fans streamed onto the park. The news from Pittodrie took an age, but confirmed that the Dons had hung on to win 1-0. A roar went up at Dens that was probably heard up at Pittodrie, for it meant that Dundee were top and needed only a point at Perth to lift the title. Pat Liney was the hero of the hour and his penalty save has entered Dens Park folklore. He must have had that lucky seal with him that night.

Liney had signed for Dundee in 1957 from junior side Dalry and altogether made 121 appearances. He debuted on the last day of 1957-58 in a 1-0 win at Ibrox and became the club's number one choice after Bill Brown's departure to Tottenham in 1959. At 5ft 10in, the wavy, dark-haired Liney was relatively small for a goalkeeper but his agility more than made up for his height.

Alan Gilzean states: 'Pat Liney's contribution to Dundee's championship season should never be underestimated and the fact that he was an ever present that year speaks for itself. He was rock solid and never let us down and it's a shame that he slipped out of the first team after we signed Bert Slater the summer after we won it.'

Bobby Wishart remembers that Liney, like Hamilton, was a great character and great to have around the dressing room, and that he fancied himself as a bit of a crooner. This was backed up at Dundee FC's Fortieth Anniversary Championship Dinner in 2002 at the Hilton Hotel in Dundee, when Liney grabbed the microphone and led the assembled Dees in a chorus of 'Hail, Hail, The Dees are Here'. Legends are made of such stuff.

And so on to Perth and arguably the greatest day in Dundee FC's history. Needing just a point, thanks to Rangers' defeat to Aberdeen, 20,000 Dundee fans made the short trip 25 miles along the Tay to see if they could realise a dream. Among them was Derek Burgess from Broughty Ferry, who had won the club's 50-50 raffle at the St Mirren match and used the money to buy a centre stand seat for the club's big day.

In Ian Ure's autobiography, he tells how he bet Alan Gilzean £10 that Gillie wouldn't score a double at Muirton. But Gillie did just that. 'I had never been so happy to lose £10,' says Ure. 'At the final whistle we stood for a moment barely aware that the honour we had fought for so hard and almost lost was at last ours.'

Dundee were Champions of Scotland. Now began their quest to become Champions of Europe.

Chapter 6

~ Continental Shockwaves ~

(May – December 1962)

The agony and the ecstasy. Dundee were Champions of Scotland, while St Johnstone were down, relegated on goal-average after a three-way tie on points at the bottom. 'No sooner had the final whistle gone than thousands of joy-crazy Dundee fans took over Muirton Park', the *Daily Record* reported on Monday, 'while thousands of dejected home fans walked quietly home.'

In Dundee the celebrations went on long and loud (although manager Bob Shankly was seen cutting his grass in his garden in Nelson Street near Dens before 9am the next day). Four times in their history Dundee had finished second in the league and now they had reached the top. Their reward was a place in the European Cup. But before the month was out they were off to New York to participate in an annual tournament normally reserved for the league runners-up.

With Rangers resurgent in the spring, the Scottish League nominated Dundee as its representatives, come what may, which meant that the new Scottish champions, rather than the Ibrox runners-up, would cross the Atlantic to compete against sides from West Germany, Brazil, Yugoslavia, Mexico and Italy.

Dundee had had very little experience of foreign opposition and Alan Gilzean remembers the tournament as providing invaluable experience for the forthcoming European Cup campaign. The six competing teams all played each other on Randall's Island. Dundee's first opponents, on 20 May, were the West German side Reutlingen. In front of a crowd of 17,500, and on a pitch littered with nuts and bolts, Dundee lost 0-2 in tropical temperatures and humidity. Dundee coaching staff constantly threw bottles of water to the players, and Gilzean remembers that at half-time none of the exhausted players looked forward to going out for the second half.

For Gordon Smith, the conditions were too much. Gilzean recalls: 'Gordon was knackered and said to us that he was going to pack it in after this and we had to persuade him that we were all just as knackered. Even at his age, Gordon was amongst the fittest players in the squad and we all struggled to cope with the heat and humidity in America.'

Dundee briefly escaped the Big Apple by flying to Detroit for a friendly against another West German side, Saarbrucken. A crowd of 5,311 saw Dundee crash 1-5, but the Scottish team learned much, for they would have to play the Germans of Cologne in the first round of the European Cup.

Ian Ure remembers that Saarbrucken gave an object lesson in possession football. 'They had so much touch and skill and would pass the ball about slowly until they reached the edge of the box, where they would tear you apart. The American thing was a real eye opener but it served us well for the European Cup and was one of the best things Bob Shankly ever did.'

Things improved back in New York. On 30 May the game against Hajduk Split of Yugoslavia ended 3-3, whereupon Dundee won their first match, 3-2, against Guadalajara of Mexico. Dundee enjoyed some unexpected backing from 70 Scots brought down from Canada by ex-Celtic goalkeeper Joe Kennaway. The ex-pats were introduced to Shankly and thanked for their support.

Dundee's next match, on 10 June, produced a 1-1 draw against Italian side Palermo. Bobby Waddell scored Dundee's goal and the youngster netted again in the final game, a 2-3 defeat to FC America of Brazil, who thereby won the tournament without a defeat to their name. The final league table was as follows:

	P	W	D	L	F	A	Pts
FC America	5	3	2	0	11	8	8
Reutlingen	5	3	1	1	6	4	7
Guadalajara	5	1	2	2	7	7	4
Palermo	5	1	2	2	7	8	4
Dundee	5	1	2	2	9	11	4
Hajduk Split	5	1	1	3	8	10	3

Overall, Bobby Wishart felt Dundee had done well, but were 'beaten by the blinking heat'. Dundee had spent almost six weeks in the USA. According to Wishart, the trip prepared them for spending time together away from home, which would benefit the team on the European Cup away legs to come. Wishart shared a room with Bobby Seith, and the players would retain the same room-mates in Europe.

One player who did not travel was Craig Brown, who spent the summer receiving treatment on his knee injury. He received a postcard from Bob Shankly which said: 'Sorry you missed the trip Craig,' a thoughtful gesture which made Brown feel he was still a part of things. In Brown's autobiography he states that as Scotland manager he made a point of sending a postcard to any player who missed a Scotland trip through injury. 'I learned that from Bob Shankly and I am sure that it has gone a long way to helping with the great team spirit we had in the Scotland camp.'

Brown also remembers that immediately after Dundee won the league Shankly went to see him to make sure he didn't feel neglected, and to give him the same bonus money as the rest of the squad. Brown says: 'It wasn't the money but the fact I was being treated the same as everyone else. I received the same bonus and – more importantly – I also received my championship medal, something which I cherish to this day.'

Now the problems began. When the party returned home from New York six of Dundee's fifteen-man championship squad refused to sign new contracts. Hamilton, Penman, Robertson, Seith, Ure and Gilzean all rejected the club's offer of £25 a week, which was a basic wage bettered at the time only by the Old Firm. One inevitable source of discontent was that when Dundee players went away on international duty, their ears were filled with dressing-room chatter about how much other players were earning in Glasgow and England.

Seith and Penman had both arrived in Dundee from English clubs, while Hamilton, Penman, Ure, Robertson and Gilzean had all played for Scotland at some level during the championship season. Their ears had pricked at the thought of what they might earn elsewhere.

The crisis was eased when, on the evening of the club's public trial, Hamilton, Penman and Robertson re-signed. The trial was then cancelled due to a 'waterlogged pitch' but, with the rain light rather than heavy, some suspected that the cancellation was due to contractual deadlock, which would have affected the two sides Dundee fielded. Thankfully, the following day Seith also signed and Gilzean and Ure followed shortly afterwards, following what Craig Brown describes as 'a storm in a teacup'. Ian Ure told the press that it was simply a matter of pounds, shillings and pence, and now I can get my dander up for Saturday's derby against United.'

As League Champions, Dundee had hoped to kick off the new season at home on a Saturday, so that they could unveil the championship flag. Instead, they were scheduled to play their first game away, at Tannadice of all places, in a League Cup sectional tie.

On the transfer front, Bob Shankly had released Ronnie Crichton, Billy McMillan and Billy Smith, who had played no part in the championship campaign, and signed left-winger Doug Houston from Queen's Park and goalkeeper Bert Slater from Liverpool for £2,500. Houston had been recommended to Shankly by Craig Brown, who knew the player through his PE studies at Jordanhill College. Slater had been admired by Shankly for a while, and had done well against Dundee in Liverpool's goal during the friendly which officially opened the Dens Park's floodlights in March 1960. Shankly had sought a goalkeeper from the start of the title season and had bid for Slater in January, but brother Bill had said no.

Most people thought Slater was coming as cover for Liney, and were taken by surprise when the former Falkirk man went straight into the side at Tannadice. Liney had been ever present in 1961-62 and is described in Norrie Price's centenary history *Up Wi' The Bonnets* as 'a steady keeper – brilliant when needed'. Jim Hendry, in *Dundee Greats,* says that 'the role of Pat Liney in that championship season should never be underestimated as he was rock solid from start to spectacular finish.'

Liney's vital penalty save against St Mirren had help establish the goal-keeper as a hero in fans' eyes. Indeed, when my father and I met him at a Dens Park Open Day in 1982, a queue of older supporters were more keen to meet Pat than on seeing the current squad. My father insisted that I obtain Liney's autograph, despite the fact that at nine years of age I was little interested in a man I knew nothing of. I was more concerned with getting the signatures of my favourites, Cammy Fraser and Peter Mackie. Liney was an obvious hero of my father, however, something which I came to appreciate years later. It seems harsh that, having played in all the games in New York, Liney returned to Scotland to find himself dropped for the first time, despite having seemingly done little wrong.

Alan Gilzean sympathises with Liney's plight and likens him to Spurs' striker Les Allen. 'There is no doubt that Pat Liney was unlucky to lose his place in the side after we won the league and it reminds me of Les Allen at Spurs, who scored over twenty goals when Tottenham won the double and then was dropped when Jimmy Greaves came back from Italy. It was neither player's fault and it just comes down to the managers making tough decisions which they felt were for the good of the team. Mind you, when you saw Bert Slater's performances in Europe and in the 1964 Cup final, you would say Shankly's decision was right, but who's to say that Pat would not have performed just as well?'

So, Pat Liney had to be content with a seat in the stand for the first game of the season. Bert Slater claimed the No 1 yellow jersey in front of a 25,300 crowd at a revamped Tannadice Park. The champions got off to the worst possible start, losing 2-3.

Dundee's League Cup section in 1962-63 was described in the match programme for the next game, at home to Celtic, as 'probably the most entertaining, though hardest of the League Cup sections. A section with

Dundee United, Celtic, Hearts and ourselves should attract fair attendances and we will have to be at our best to qualify.'

As Celtic's visit constituted Dundee's first home match of the season, the Championship flag was duly unfurled, according to a tradition that continues to this day. A special flagpole was erected behind the goal at the TC Keay East end and was unveiled by Lady Provost McManus just before the teams emerged to a tumultuous roar.

That same flag fluttered at Dens on matchdays – on a pole at the east end of the main grandstand – until 1991, when it was deemed to be too weather-beaten. Astonishingly, new chairmen Ron Dixon, who took over in January 1992, undertook a massive clear-out at Dens and even disposed of the flag! Luckily, Dundee fan Alan Smith spotted it in a bin outside Dens and rescued it. He returned it to the club a few years later, once the new board of Peter and Jimmy Marr had taken control. The flag now graces a wall-frame in the concourse of the Bobby Cox Stand, enabling a new generation of Dundee supporters to admire the biggest prize the club has ever won.

The players were still in the dressing room prior to the Celtic game, and therefore were denied a sight of the flag being raised. Interestingly, they never saw the actual trophy arrive at Dens either, as there was no official ceremony. Alan Gilzean remembers seeing the trophy for the first time when it adorned the boardroom on 6 August, the date of the scheduled public trial. It was not until three days later that the players got their first proper look at it, during an official photo call, when a new strip was also unveiled. Instead of the dark blue, V-neck, long-sleeved strip of the championship season, the club would kick off the new campaign with a round neck, short-sleeve top, although it retained the distinctive badge in a shield. (The badge remained the same until 1969-70, when it was changed from a shield to a circle. The shield design returned on Dundee's First Division winning strip in 1998 and on a variety of away strips. The championship-style badge returned for the 2003 Scottish Cup final, and was retained for a specially commissioned UEFA Cup strip to mark Dundee's return to Europe after a 29-year absence.)

A healthy 21,000 crowd turned up to watch the flag unfurled and they were treated to a thrilling League Cup-tie against Celtic in which Dundee recorded their first win of the season. Gordon Smith, whom the press doubted would survive another full year at the top – but who would make 48 appearances – scored the only goal.

On the final whistle, hundreds of young Dundee supporters invaded the pitch. Dens Park had witnessed several pitch invasions the year before, most notably in the final home game against St Mirren, but the club was no longer prepared to tolerate them. After repeated warnings in the match programme and over the tannoy, the club decided that juveniles would not get into the next match, against Hearts, for a reduced admission price. A club spokesman told the *Courier*: 'We have given repeated warnings about this business and we have decided to act to curb it. There will no boys' gate on Saturday, but this will not affect the pensioners' gate.'

The ban didn't affect the size of the crowd, which numbered 20,000, and most left disappointed as Dundee crashed 0-2. With two defeats in three games, qualification for Dundee was already a tall order. They had a chance for revenge four days later at Tynecastle, when the Dees opened the defence of their title, but the Jam Tarts ran out 3-1 winners.

Hearts had become the 'hammer' of the Dundee clubs, according to *The Scotsman*, for in their last three games they had beaten Dundee twice and Dundee United once. The *Courier* noted that Dundee missed Gilzean, out with a knee injury, and 'without him the forwards seem to carry not an ounce of punch'.

The day after the Tynecastle defeat, the Dundee City Council staged a civic reception in honour of Dundee's championship win, held in the Dundee City Chambers in the City Square. The reception consisted of a dinner and speeches by the Lord Provost, the local MP and by Dundee's chairman James Gellatly.

The atmosphere, however, was more subdued than when the players had been honoured in the same place after the Muirton win in April. The team had now lost three times in four games, several players had only re-signed after difficult contract negotiations, and one of them – Andy Penman – had demanded a transfer, following a frank exchange of views between players and coaching staff at training.

Spirits were lifted two days later when Dundee beat Dundee United 2-1 to keep their faint qualification hopes alive. In goal for United that day was future Dundee boss Donald Mackay. During the game, Dees fans chanted 'We want Penman', whose transfer demand had become public knowledge. Soon afterwards the 19-year-old withdrew his request.

The draw for the preliminary round of the European Champions Cup had just been made. Dundee were paired with Cologne, with whom they had to agree suitable dates. There were no fixed dates in those days, only windows in which games must be completed. However, as first out of the hat, Dundee would host the Germans in the first leg, on Wednesday, 5 September, with the return leg three weeks later.

With Dundee's next outing at Celtic in the League Cup, Cologne general manager Karl Frohlich flew to Glasgow, but saw little in the Dees' performance to worry him, as Celtic won 3-0 to put the final nail in Dundee's qualification prospects. Four days later Frohlich saw nothing to make him change his assessment, as Dundee went down 0-2 at Hearts. In between, he stayed in the North British Hotel in Dundee and visited Dens to check out the facilities.

Frohlich sent a glowing report about Dundee FC's hospitality and facilities, but what about the team? He diplomatically told the *Courier* that he thought Dundee 'were bluffing'. As for Hearts, they won the section, reached their second final in a row, but this time beat Kilmarnock 1-0 to lift the trophy.

It was crushing blow for Dundee to have lost three times to the Jam Tarts by the first day of September, particularly as Hearts had finished sixteen points behind them the previous season. Dundee suffered the ignominy of finishing bottom of their section, and with no goals in their last two games, confidence was hardly high for the visit of Cologne.

In 1962 the European Cup was still in its infancy, having first been contested in 1955-56. Only two clubs – Real Madrid (the first five years) and Benfica (the last two) – had so far won it. Both these giants were in the draw for 1962-63, Real Madrid as Spanish champions and Benfica as European Cup holders. They, along with Dundee's opponents, Cologne, were installed as favourites, so Dundee could hardly have received a more difficult draw.

Dundee were only the fourth Scottish club to enter the Champions Cup, following Hibs, Rangers and Hearts. From the Dundee squad, only Gordon Smith had experience in the European Cup, having played for both Edinburgh clubs. He wore green when Hibs (rather than champions Aberdeen) were invited to compete in the inaugural competition in 1955-56. Hibs and Gordon Smith reached the semi-finals, where they lost to Rheims of France. He wore maroon in 1960-61, when Hearts lost in the preliminary round to Benfica. Dundee's entry would allow Smith to compete for a record third time with a different club.

For Bobby Wishart, however, it was a belated chance to play in a competition which had been denied to him when Aberdeen weren't put forward in 1956. Wishart says that Aberdeen were not fully aware at the time of the significance of not playing in the first European Cup, but by the time Dundee qualified seven years later it was firmly established as the premier European cup competition.

It was going to be tough for the Dark Blues, however. Not only were Cologne one of the favourites, but Dundee's own form was miserable. The German party arrived in Dundee on the Monday evening, minus inside-forward Ernst Habig, who hated flying and was making his own travel arrangements. Among the party was Yugoslav manager Zlato Cajkovski and Hungarian masseur Josef Bocsai. Cajkovski explained to the media in mangled English: 'Cologne will win as our defensive football is decadent.'

The Scottish press loved it and wrote banner headlines around the remarks to whip up a frenzy. Cajkovski, according to Tommy Gallacher, was 'an impressive little character who is the complete boss with the German club though not a hard taskmaster'.

Cajkovski certainly had a good footballing pedigree, having been capped 37 times by Yugoslavia and played for the Rest of Europe against England at Wembley in 1953. He originally joined Cologne in 1955 from Partizan Belgrade and played for them for three years before coaching in Israel, Turkey and Holland. He returned to Cologne in 1961 as manager and in his first year led them to the German championship for the first time in their history.

Although interest in the game in Dundee was huge, journalist Patrick Barclay recalls that 'trepidation kept the crowd down to about 25,000', of which 140 had travelled over from Cologne. The visiting contingent took up a whole section of the main stand and were colourful to behold, with their flags, banners and toy trumpets. Seven youngsters wore white shirts which spelled out 'Cologne'. The team was also boosted by the arrival of German tank crews training at Castlemartin tank ranges in Wales.

The Cologne team boasted no fewer than ten West German internationals. Skipper Hans Schafer had been his country's outside-left when they won the World Cup in Switzerland in 1954, while left-back Karl-Heinz Schnellinger was named in the World Best XI in the 1962 World Cup in Chile, and would play in the 1966 final.

Cajkovski passed up the chance to train at Dens Park under floodlights and instead the team trained on Tuesday morning at a junior ground in the city. At the ensuing press conference he announced: 'We will attack Dundee and win. We won the championship with an aggressive and intelligent game and won't change that now.'

To commemorate the occasion, DC Thomson produced a special *Evening Telegraph* pictorial souvenir. With Dundee not then producing their own match programme for midweek matches, it became a substitute for the club's publication.

The Dundee programme had remained much the same since the mid-1950s, as an eight-page publication. The picture on the front was the same, week in, week out, and featured a photograph taken from the corner of the ground at the Dens Road-Provost Road end. It was taken under floodlights on the terracing, and looked diagonally over the ground across the south enclosure and the pitch. Not until 1966 was a different image employed.

The programme's content was basic. The two teams appeared in the centrefold, surrounded by local adverts. An editorial stretched across pages 2, 3, 7, and 8, in between more ads. Page 6 had a list of other games being played in Scotland that day. It was dubbed the 'half time scoreboard' and contained a space in which to write the scores when they were announced over the tannoy at the interval. There were no pen pictures of the opponents, although they featured in other programmes at the time, and no address from the manager. In short, it was hardly worth the 3d (about 1p) that it cost.

The pictorial souvenir for the Cologne game was a different matter altogether, and was full of colour and content that quickly made it a much sought after collectable. Costing sixpence (2½p), it was available in newsagents and shops around the city and featured on the front page a colour photo of the players with the league championship trophy.

The twelve pages provided masses of detail about both Dundee and Cologne and featured detailed pen pictures of both clubs. There were colour photos of both squads across the centre pages, plus a message from the chairman on page three. Such was the success of this publication that it was repeated for all of Dundee's home European Cup ties that season, and again for various big matches for both city clubs over the next twenty years.

Another change Dundee made for the game concerned their strip, for they had reverted to the long-sleeved V-neck top with which they had won the league. The players apparently associated the new round-neck, short-sleeved version with their poor start to 1962-63 and asked to switch back again. In view of the remarkable result that was about to unfold, the round-neck strip was abandoned for good!

So the scene was set for Dundee's first foray into European football, and when the teams came out together, led by a pipe band playing 'Up Wi' The Bonnets', they were greeted to a tumultuous roar. Bobby Cox led out his team to the TC Keay end, as this was the traditional 'home' end. Even after the introduction of segregation in the 1970s, Dundee still liked to run to the east end of the ground, although it had by then been allocated as the terracing for the away support, and that tradition remained until only recently.

The Dundee team that lined up for the national anthems was experienced. Although Craig Brown, Alec Stuart, Doug Houston and Kenny Cameron had all played in the first seven games of 1962-63, against Cologne Shankly reverted to the eleven which had served so well in the title success. The only exception was in goal, where Bert Slater made a European debut denied to Pat Liney. The only other time that eleven had played together in the new season, Dundee had beaten Celtic 1-0.

According to Ian Ure, European Cup veteran Gordon Smith helped plan the tactics, as 'he had the vital experience which is so necessary to any side competing in a top competition.' Immediately from the kick-off Dundee poured forward in numbers. In the second minute Alan Cousin 'collided' with the German keeper Fritz Ewart, who was laid out cold for a few minutes before groggily returning to his place.

Ewart didn't have much time to recover. Seven minutes later German centre-back Hemmersbach was pressurised into heading Andy Penman's cross into his own net. Two minutes later Dundee doubled their lead with a goal described by Craig Brown as one of the most extraordinary he had ever seen. From the edge of the box Bobby Wishart miscued, the ball trundled one way, a huge divot flew the other, and Ewart dived to save the divot. The German goalkeeper ended up with turf in his hands and the ball in the net behind him.

'I still remember Wishart's goal in that Cologne game,' Dundee fan Eddie Rattray from Menzieshill told me. 'As their keeper dived the wrong way to save a divot from Bobby's boot, the ball rolled into the net. Half the crowd thought at first he'd saved it and didn't know what had happened and it seemed unreal that we were two up so early.'

It was three a minute later, thanks to Hugh Robertson, who fired in off Regh, Gilzean made it four when he headed home a Smith cross, and Smith added a fifth, all before half-time. As Craig Brown says: 'It was a half-time scoreline which must have sent shockwaves around Europe and emotions were very high at the interval.'

The match was being broadcast live on BBC Radio, with commentary from Kenneth Wolstenholme, and there were reports the next day of the cheers being heard as far away as the city centre, a mile away. Current Dundee Chief Executive Peter Marr recalled before the current team's 2003 UEFA Cup home tie with KS Vllaznia of Albania how special that Cologne game had been.

For the second half Cologne were down to ten men. Goalkeeper Ewart did not reappear and right-back Tony Regh took over in goal. So dazed was Ewart that in the dressing room at half-time he thought the score was 2-0 and that the game was over.

More goals were therefore bound to come. Penman headed in from close range, and by now every Dundee goal prompted dancing on the terracing and on the track. The excitement communicated itself to ticketless spectators outside the ground, and the arm-waving fans at the top of the

Dens Road and Provost Road terracings semaphored the score to people on the pavements outside.

Gilzean made it seven with a bullet header from Hamilton's cross, and Gillie completed his hat-trick when he headed in a centre from Alan Cousin. Eight goals, and only 67 minutes played. At this rate it could have ended up twelve or more. Instead, it was the Germans who scored the only remaining goal, Hamilton turning a Habig cross into his own net. At the other end, Cajkovski was ordered away from behind the goal, presumably for coaching his stand-in keeper.

The Dundee players sportingly lined up at the tunnel to applaud the Cologne players off, while they themselves were shortly greeted by a mass of autograph hunters at the players' entrance, despite the rain now beginning to fall. Inevitably, swarms of small and not so small boys had poured onto the pitch at the final whistle, and perhaps the only level-headed person in the ground was Bob Shankly. His reaction was typically low key: 'I am delighted, but the boys rose to the occasion as I expected them to. Naturally this puts us in a very strong position for the return but we won't be letting up.'

Shankly could take personal satisfaction from the result. Following the New York tournament in May he had intended switching from a 2-3-5 formation to 4-2-4, but the idea was scrapped after the reserves (in 2-3-5) had repeatedly beaten the first team in practice. The intention had been for Seith and Ure to play in central defence, with Penman falling back to right-half. In the event, the 2-3-5 formation was retained for the Cologne match and it paid dividends as Dundee recorded 23 shots on goal to Cologne's six.

'It was easily our best performance since we beat the Swedish champions Elfsborg 8-1, and the boys were great', Shankly added, still managing, according to the *Courier,* 'to look his usual imperturbable self.'

But for the unhappy team from the city on the banks of the Rhine, it was a case of 'woe to vanquished' as they suffered a club record defeat that stands to this day. The Cologne party who attended the aftermatch banquet in a city centre hotel looked a disconsolate bunch, and secretary Karl Frohlich admitted: 'We have no excuses. We had plans to beat Dundee but we just didn't use them. For one thing, they were supposed to go into the tackle quickly but instead they kept falling back. We will win in Cologne, however, but we have no chance of winning the tie.'

Trouble was brewing, however. Cologne had been so humiliated that they left Scotland muttering threats of retaliation in the second leg. Manager Zlato Cajkovski told the German press that the result of the second leg might be different 'if, say, the Dundee goalkeeper was injured'.

A photograph then appeared in German newspapers which looked as if Alan Cousin had deliberately laid out Fritz Ewart with a punch.

From a certain angle it looked like a punch had been thrown, but journalist Patrick Barclay says he would have 'sworn on his Wee Red Book that Cousin was incapable of hurting anyone on purpose'. He wrote in 1987 that Cousin was notable for two things: his double shuffle, which left defenders floundering, and an absence of malice. Photos taken from a different angle confirmed that no punch had been thrown.

Alan himself says it was an accident, but the press used the damning photo, not the other one, to whip up anti-Dundee sentiment among the German public. One thing which must be considered is that the Dundee v Cologne match took place just eighteen years after the War, when it would have been easy for the German press to whip up anti-British feeling. Many supporters of both clubs would have been young enough to have fought in the War, or had friends or relatives who had lost their lives. This was, after all, one the first competitive ties between German and British club sides.

Cologne were looking for scapegoats, and by the time Dundee lined up in the Mungerdorf Stadium three weeks later the home crowd were baying for blood. Dundee were naive when they travelled to Germany, according to Craig Brown, while Gilzean describes the tie in Cologne as 'experiencing the highs and lows of European football'. No sooner had they arrived than Dundee started to encounter problems over accommodation and over training facilities, all of which they innocently attributed to language difficulties.

The pitch they were due to train on was rutted and holed, while the hotel didn't have enough rooms to accommodate the Dundee party. On the night of the match, however, matters boiled over when Dundee directors and officials were shunned by their German counterparts and had to find their own seats in the stadium. Dundee secretary Bob Crichton said upon his return that 'the Cologne chairman completely ignored us before the game and we were left at half-time without even an offer of a cup of tea and after the match we were again ignored'.

It was little better for the small band of Dundee supporters who had accompanied Dundee on a charter flight organised by Dickson's Travel in Reform Street, for they found themselves pushed and jostled on their way into the ground. My father was among the Dundee supporters, as he happened to be working for a short while in Germany at the time. He described the atmosphere as frightening and intimidating. The players sensed the same and Ian Ure describes in *Dundee Greats* how half of his team-mates 'bottled it and lost all their shape and form'.

Things appeared ominous from the kick-off, when stretcher-bearers took up position behind Bert Slater's goal. Ure says: 'Slater was a definite target from the start.'

Cologne had a billy-goat mascot, which trotted out at every home game, named Hennes ('Little John'). Hennes was considered a good omen and was incorporated into the badge on the team's shirts. Cologne, however, needed more than luck if they were going to overturn a seven-goal deficit but, backed by 40,000 horn-blowing fans, they were going to give it their best shot.

They got the perfect start. Alex Hamilton punched a Schafer header over the bar, and inside-left Ernst-Gunther Habig converted the penalty. Midway through the half, Dundee's worst fears were realised. Slater was caught by Mueller's boot when diving for a low ball. With blood oozing from behind his ear, Slater had to be led off, replaced in goal by Andy Penman.

'Whoever made the call to put Andy in the goal has made better decisions', Ian Ure claims, for he quickly conceded two goals to give the Germans a 3-0 half-time lead.' The Dundee dressing room at half-time was in disarray, and Ure reckons that Dundee were in real danger of losing the tie: 'If it wasn't for Bobby Cox, Bert Slater and myself, we might have gone out, cos we tried to hold it together while others lost it. If we hadn't, it could have been 10-0 to Cologne as we didn't battle as hard as we should have.'

Shankly tried to calm his irate players, who were so incensed at the treatment from the Germans that Gilzean called their tactics 'diabolical'. Gordon Smith, in particular, was singled out for some rough treatment, and he came into the dressing room with his legs black and blue.

The worst treatment, of course, had been dished out to Bert Slater, whom the German medics had tried to get into an ambulance and on to hospital. Slater refused and entered the dressing room at half-time. According to Craig Brown, Slater diffused the situation by making a joke describing himself as looking like Lana Turner with his head wrapped in a turban-like bandage.

Slater declared his willingness to resume, but it was decided not to risk him in goal, so instead he agreed to play out on the wing. (He would later describe himself as a better winger than Gordon Smith – 'another example of the legendary Slater wit', says Brown.)

When Ian Ure shortly deflected the ball into his own net, to make it 4-0, Dundee were in real danger of capsizing. If they had, says Paddy Barclay, 'it would have remained the most radical transformation in two-legged football to this day.'

The jitters were so bad that Slater did, after all, go back in goal. He proved to be a turban-mopped inspiration, but even he was powerless when Cologne soon got a second penalty. It was a pivotal moment. Had it gone in, the Germans would have needed only two more goals, and 30 minutes in which to get them, to force a third match 'replay'. ('Away goals' in Europe were not introduced until 1967.) Instead, Habig drove his kick against the crossbar, and with it went Cologne's hopes of the greatest turnaround in European football.

According to Gilzean, 'Punchy [Slater] and big Ian were immense that night and if it wasn't for them we could have gone out. Bert played a blinder in Europe and in that Cologne game he was simply brilliant.'

As the minutes ticked away, and the German crowd accepted the inevitable, they began encircling the pitch, massing along the touchline. Gordon Smith was tripped by a spectator as he ran down the line, and Ure says that 'at any moment I was expecting to be engulfed by a screaming mob'.

At the end, Dundee were 'saved by a miracle', says Ure. Hundreds of off-duty British Army servicemen from the Rhine Army, at the game to support Dundee, threw a cordon around the team to get them off the pitch unhurt – or practically unhurt.

Ian Ure and Bobby Cox were struck on the legs by foldaway chairs wielded by German fans, while Andy Penman and Bobby Wishart took a kicking as they left the park. Gordon Smith had to be helped off by two of his team-mates as he could hardly walk.

Bert Slater had had two stitches in his head but, perhaps worst of all, from a sporting point of view, was the behaviour of the Cologne players who, back in their dressing room before the Dundee squad, threw tumblers of water over their opponents as they passed to go to their own.

Gordon Smith, with 22 years of experience at every level of football, admitted that he had 'never played in a dirtier game. It may not have been apparent from the sidelines but most of their fouls were committed when the ball was away.' Bob Shankly contented himself by saying 'I have seen a lot of European Cup-ties in my day but that was the most brutal of all. I can't understand why the referee allowed so many of those incidents to take place.'

At the instigation of the players, the party opted to dispense with the official reception and return to their own hotel for a meal. Vice-chairman Jack Swadel said: 'Dundee in the past have toured in several countries but we have never been so insulted as we have been tonight.'

Rebuffed by the Dundee players, Cologne therefore invited the visiting supporters to the banquet instead. My father was among those who went. He described how everyone was completely ignored and made to feel most unwelcome, but they at least got some free food and drink which 'no self-respecting Dundonian would turn down'.

My father would never forget his trip to Cologne. He bought a Dundee scarf for the purpose, which I inherited when he passed away. He had bought it from Cairds in Reform Street in Dundee, and wore it to every match he attended for the next 40 years. Dad used to talk about Dundee's European adventures, which are favourite stories amongst the supporters and, as the club had last played in Europe in 1974, I promised Dad that I would take the scarf abroad with me when Dundee next qualified. I fulfilled that pledge when, after a 29-year absence, Dundee returned to the UEFA Cup in 2003 and I travelled with the scarf to watch them against Albanian side KS Vllaznia.

But for those at Cologne on 26 September 1962, there were bitter memories tinged with relief, for Dundee had progressed into the next round with an 8-5 aggregate win.

'After those ugly, frightening scenes,' wrote Ian Ure in the *All Stars Football Book* in 1963, 'I felt sickened by the continent. I began to wonder if the European Cup was worth risking serious injury in brawling battles which were little to do with football, but we were then drawn against Portugal's Sporting Club and all my fears disappeared again.'

Bert Slater's defiance in Germany gave the Dark Blue faithful a new hero between the sticks. Slater had joined Dundee for £2,500 in July from Bob Shankly's brother, Bill's, Liverpool, for whom he had played a big part in Liverpool's promotion surge. He had joined the Reds in June 1959 from Falkirk in a swap deal for Tommy Younger, and he been capped for Scotland at Under-23 level while at Brockville and toured Denmark with the full Scotland team in 1959.

At 5ft 9in, with short, light brown hair tousled at the front, Slater was small for a goalkeeper but he was one of the most agile in the game. He was nicknamed Punchy by his team-mates because he looked like a wee boxer, with so many thick ears and scars from kicks about the face. But Ian Ure described him as a 'hard, hard man'.

Slater's Dundee career saw him make 101 appearances between 1962 and 1965. He would become renowned not only for his performance in Cologne, but also for the 1964 Scottish Cup final, which has become nicknamed 'The Bert Slater final'. Although Dundee lost 1-3 to Rangers, two injury-time goals distorted the outcome. Slater had almost single-handedly defied Rangers until the dying seconds.

Not surprisingly, following his battering in Cologne, Slater was in no fit shape to face Rangers three days later, and Pat Liney resumed the duties. The Scottish international selectors were at Ibrox to weigh up Ian Ure. Dundee held Rangers to a 1-1 draw to extend their unbeaten league run at Ibrox to six years, and Ure must have felt confident of adding to his two full caps.

That was Dundee's fifth league game. They were in mid-table – posting draws against Aberdeen and Dundee United and beaten Clyde – and in mid-table they remained for the rest of the campaign. That mattered little while Dundee were a conquering force in Europe, and supporters' minds had more distant horizons. But before the next round Dundee had to face Falkirk on 6 October at Dens. Bizarrely, before the match kicked off, the referee had his coin 'stolen' by two charity collectors who rushed up after he had tossed it, grabbed it from the grass, tossed it into their tin and dashed off. They were raising money for Dundee's homeless, but didn't do it as a pre-determined charity stunt and were chased by the police. Only when the constables realised what had happened did they give up the chase. The collectors were allowed back onto the terracing without facing arrest. Dundee duly chalked up their second home win, 2-1, but they were still down in eighth position.

All thoughts, however, were on the European Cup draw the following Monday. It paired the Dark Blues with the Portuguese champions Sporting Club of Lisbon. Portugal had two clubs in the European Cup that season; the other was Benfica, the holders.

The first leg was arranged for Lisbon on 24 October, with the return just seven days later. During Dundee's home game with Kilmarnock, Sporting manager Armando Ferreira was an interested spectator. The Dees won 1-0 to extend their unbeaten league run to seven matches and lift them to within four points of leaders Hearts. Ferreira appeared to be impressed, and although he told the press he thought Sporting could win, he thought Dundee would provide a stern test. He was particularly impressed by Bobby Cox, Gordon Smith and Alan Gilzean, and he confessed to being surprised by the pace of the game in Scotland.

Following the Kilmarnock win, 17,000 tickets were sold for the home leg, with the queue stretching well beyond Tannadice. Missing from the team that day were Alex Hamilton and Ian Ure, on duty with Scotland in Cardiff where they both earned caps in a 3-2 win against Wales. The players met up with their team-mates in London on the Monday.

The final of the European Cup in 1962-63 had initially been earmarked for Wembley. But now there was talk of UEFA decreeing that if English champions Ipswich or Scottish champions Dundee reached the final, it would be switched elsewhere, probably Paris. It is curious that UEFA deemed Wembley to be a non-neutral venue for a Scottish club, and, indeed, after Ipswich were knocked out at an early stage nothing more was heard of the planned change. Wembley awaited Dundee, provided they got there. It all seemed a fuss about nothing, because two years later, in 1965, AC Milan would win the European Cup final – in Milan!

Whatever the venue, the prospect of Dundee reaching the final was a distant one as they headed out to Portugal. Sporting Club had been formed in 1906. The club's activities encompassed football, athletics, tennis, cycling, badminton, squash, motor cycle and motor racing. Their stadium was amongst the most impressive in Europe, with a 60,000 capacity. Sporting's football achievements included eleven national championships and five Portuguese Cups. Their squad was an array of international talent from Portugal and Brazil.

Hugh Robertson was out through injury, but otherwise Dundee were at full strength. Around 100 fans made the trip and were among a crowd of 50,000. The kick-off was delayed to allow photographs of the two captains shaking hands and exchanging pennants. The game, according to Tommy Gallacher, was 'one of the fastest, most gruelling but sportiest European Cup-ties ever seen'.

Dundee conceded a last-minute goal in a melee which saw the ball cleared from just behind the line. In celebration the Portuguese crowd tossed into the air their soft cushions, which then cascaded down onto the pitch. Gilzean admitted that Sporting had deserved their lead, but thought they looked a small side which Dundee could get the better of at Dens. Searching for new heroes, the *Courier* said that Wishart's performance had been his best game in his Dundee career.

A week later, a full-strength Dundee, with Robertson restored, were roared on by a 32,000 Dens Park crowd to a 4-1 win which would send the Dees through 4-2 on aggregate.

Fans had arrived at Dens a good two hours before kick-off, and no car parking spaces could be found for miles around. The difficulties in parking were accentuated by the fact that Gussie Park behind Dens was being used for a carnival, and a force of fourteen traffic police were stationed to cope with the thousands of motor cars which arrived. As kick-off approached, drivers had to look further afield. Clepington Road from Strathmartine Road to North Court Street was jammed solid on both sides and all side-streets leading off were crowded.

Late-comers missed Dundee's opening goal on thirteen minutes, scored by Gilzean, to level the tie. Sporting proved to be a skilful side prone to over-elaboration near goal. On half-time Alan Cousin headed Smith's cross in off the underside of the bar to put Dundee ahead at a crucial time. Gordon Smith was at his best, according to Bobby Wishart, 'the most cultured player afield'. In the second half Smith set up Dundee's third goal and played a part in the fourth, both put away by Alan Gilzean.

At 4-1, there appeared no way back for the Portuguese team. They managed to claw one goal back, but Dundee proudly took their place in the last eight of the European Cup. The other seven were AC Milan, Dukla Prague, Benfica, Feyenoord, Rheims, Galatasaray and Anderlecht.

'Those European nights were special,' recalls Gilzean. Ian Ure felt that the games against Sporting were 'the best possible advert for European tournaments. Both games were the same – not a single angry incident and very few fouls.'

With his second European hat-trick of the season, Gilzean was once again being praised to the skies. He was proving that, despite not yet being a full international, he could cut it at the highest level in Europe. Signed for Dundee by Willie Thornton in 1957, Gillie would go on to become one of the greatest players in the history of the club, playing 173 times and scoring 160 goals. He won a Scottish championship medal with Dundee, played in a European Cup semi-final, a Scottish Cup final, and earned five of his 22 full international caps as a Dundee player. Despite hailing from nearby Coupar Angus, Gilzean was not a Dundee fan as a boy, lavishing his affection on Hibs' famous forward line. 'My father used to take me to Dens when Hibs came to visit and Gordon Smith was a big hero of mine,' Gillie says, 'and so it was a great thrill to play alongside him when he signed for Dundee. I never imagined that happening as a kid kicking a ball about.'

Gilzean was the last Dundee player to do his National Service while at the club. During his last six months in the Army he would travel up by train on Thursday nights from his base in Aldershot.

After banging in the goals for the reserves, Gilzean made his first-team debut on 22 August 1959 in a 1-4 League Cup defeat at home to Motherwell. By the end of that season he had scored eight goals in eight league appearances.

Standing 5ft 9in, with short, dark hair, Gilzean quickly became the answer to Dundee's goalscoring problems and by 1960-61 he was a regular in the line up, scoring 32 goals in 42 matches. Gillie is Dundee's all-time highest goalscorer and also holds the record for the most goals in one season, when he scored an incredible 52 in 1963-64, his last season at the club.

Playing mostly at inside-left for Dundee, wearing the No 10 shirt, Gilzean had a tremendous shot and a great finishing prowess, plus heading ability for which he became famed. He was able to spring high above defenders and was described in the Dundee's European Cup quarter-final match programme in 1963 as 'the best header in Scotland'.

Gilzean was a hero not just for Dundee, however, but also for Scotland. He scored the goal in a 1-0 win over England at Hampden in 1964 while a Dundee player. Indeed, in the same year Gilzean became the last Dundee player to score for Scotland before Lee Wilkie headed the winner against Iceland in March 2003.

In Jim Crumley's *The Road and the Miles: A Homage to Dundee*, a whole chapter is dedicated to hero-worship of Gillie. He describes the championship side as 'a team of many felicities and distinctions and at number ten, one phenomenon'. Every schoolboy wannabe footballer in Dundee in the early 1960s wanted to be Alan Gilzean, and the number of goals a Gilzean impersonator scored in the city's back greens and streets must reach into the tens of thousands.

Gilzean himself set a personal goalscoring milestone when, in a 10-2 massacre of Queen of the South in December 1962, he netted seven, equalling Bert Juliussen's club record of seven goals in one match set in 1947. It was just one short of Jimmy McGrory's Scottish record of eight goals in one game for Celtic in 1928.

Two days after the Queens win, the draw for the European Cup paired Dundee with Belgian champions Anderlecht, who had knocked out Real Madrid in the first round. The European adventure, however, was taking its toll on Dundee's domestic form. An alarming slump saw them lose to Dunfermline, Partick and Third Lanark. The Thirds defeat was a particular embarrassment as the Dundee players could be seen arguing and shouting at each other as they went into the Cathkin dressing room at half-time, 1-4 down. Disgruntled fans were by now barracking some of the players and, in particular, Bert Slater whose kicking was coming under scrutiny from the terracing. Despite wins in December against Queens, St Mirren and Raith Rovers, by New Year Dundee found themselves nine points behind leaders Rangers and the defence of their championship looked in tatters.

Gilzean, however, told the Dundee supporters who shared the train home with the players from Kirkcaldy on 22 December that Dundee could still catch Rangers. But the reality, according to Dundee historian Norrie Price, was that 'gone was the rapier-like play which had earlier destroyed Cologne and Sporting'.

With the European Cup quarter-finals against Anderlecht not due until March, Dundee had time to recover the scintillating form which had deserted them. With the league slipping slowly from Dundee's grasp, it looked like a cup run was going to be their only chance of glory.

Chapter 7

~ So Near And Yet So Far ~

(January – May 1963)

1963 promised much for the citizens of Dundee. There was the continued expansion and redevelopment of the city centre, a visit to the city by The Beatles scheduled for October, and for supporters of Dundee FC the start of a Scottish Cup campaign and a European Cup quarter-final to whet the appetite.

By the time the Fab Four arrived they were almost as famous locally as the footballers from Dens Park. Several of the players were able to go backstage after the concert to meet John, Paul, George and Ringo. When the Liverpool quartet arrived they were top of the charts with 'She Loves You'. In its review of the concert, the *Courier* remarked that 'if Bob Shankly could get the same vocal support for the Dark Blues, Dundee would be in the same position in the football world as The Beatles are in Tin Pan Alley'.

The year didn't start on the pitch as well as it might, however. Dundee lost the New Year north-east derby 0-1 at Aberdeen, and went down 2-3 at Clyde four days later. New Year's Day in Scotland was traditionally derby day. Rangers played Celtic, Hibs took on Hearts and – with Dundee United languishing in the Second Division – Pittodrie was the nearest to a local derby for Dundee. United's promotion in 1960 had no effect on this tradition, and Dundee continued to face Aberdeen on 1 January into the 1990s. Nowadays, derby days are all but lost to Scottish football but, since they returned to the Premier League in 1998, Dundee still tend to play Aberdeen around the festive season.

For one Dundee player, however, 1963 started brightly. Ian Ure was presented with the Scottish Footballer of the Year Award for 1962, chosen by Rex Kingsley of the *Sunday Mail.* The Kingsley award had been presented annually since 1951, when Hibs' Gordon Smith won it. It predated the Scottish Football Writers' Player of the Year (introduced in 1965) and the Scottish Professional Footballers Association Player of the Year (1978).

Ure was the twelfth winner of the 'Kingsley', previous holders having included former Dundee manager Willie Thornton (1952). Kingsley announced his decision in the *Sunday Mail* on Sunday, 30 December with the words: 'I am happy to name Ian Ure, Dundee and Scotland's blond giant centre half, as my footballer of the year, 1962. Especially happy because a job, which sometimes in the past has given me much concern and worry, proved one of the most simple in years. Ian Ure stands out like the bow of a naval destroyer. The honour could have gone to none other. For this Herculean 23-year-old has so drilled himself in the soccer arts, by punishing voluntary training and relentless mastering of the ball, that his growth and football stature is almost breathtaking. I question if in Britain there is a finer stop-and-start pivot in the business – stopping the goal hunger of the enemy and feeding the same hunger in his own forward mates. No wonder Ian Ure is the idol of Dens Park – and of Scots everywhere when he appears in a national jersey.'

A presentation ceremony was held in Caird Hall on Sunday, 24 February, and the evening was well attended by the press and members of Dundee FC Supporters Association. Entertainment was provided by the Alexander Brothers from television's White Heather Club, and The Cortina Group (the Dundee Supporters Club Resident Band) and by Ure's team-mate Pat Liney. A souvenir programme marked the event, in which manager Bob Shankly gave the following tribute:

'We at Dens Park were absolutely delighted when we opened the *Sunday Mail* at the end of the year to read that Rex had chosen our centre-half, Ian Ure, as his Player of the Year, 1962. To use an old expression, it couldn't have happened to a better fellow. On reflection, however, it would have been difficult for Rex to have overlooked such an outstanding personality in our game. Ian Ure is not only a highly skilled player – he is a morale builder in any side, club or national. Like successful men in any sphere of life, Ian hates to lose. Thus, his virtues as a team-mate are never more noticeable than when the battle is at its toughest. His very presence, as he races to cover every possible leak, or nails the ball to stab it forward to a mate, means much to his colleagues on the field. This determination to turn defence into attack by the skill and physique, with which he has been blessed, sometimes makes him a shade unpopular at away games. But that doesn't worry Ian – indeed he might think he is playing a poor game if the enemy didn't think him worth a raspberry! Here is a man who never accepts defeat – indeed some of his greatest performances have been in a losing side, as against Cologne in Germany in the European Cup, when, despite much provocation, he kept his head and helped to keep the side in the competition. I say frankly that in all my experience as a player and manager, I have never come across one who thrashed himself so hard to reach the top, returning to Dens Park time and time again to slave at mastering the ball on his own. With average luck, Ian Ure will continue to play an important part in our game, at club and national level.'

Ian Ure therefore became the first and, to date, only Dundee player to win a national Player of the Year Award (other than divisional awards). His performances both home and abroad had certainly merited it, as the 6ft 1in sheet anchor had become one of the outstanding defenders in the country. He had signed for Dundee in 1958 from his local under-18 side Ayr Albion, after being spotted by Dundee scout Jimmy Ross. After just four months in the reserves he made his debut for the first team in a 3-2 home win over Falkirk. Ure had signed as a left-half, and in his first game his direct opponent was a future Spurs legend. Ure recalls: 'I was supposed to mark John White of Falkirk and I never found him that day. He seemed to shoot up out of the drainage holes the groundsman had made with his fork.'

At school, Ure had excelled at rugby and he was reared by his school, Ayr Academy, as a stand off. He played for the 1st XV at just sixteen and maintains that as most of his opponents were bigger than him, he had to battle for every ball, which helped him build his mighty frame.

Ure didn't ignore football, however, as he played for Ayr Albion on Saturday afternoons after playing rugby for the school in the mornings. At seventeen he was capped for the Scottish Boys Club against England and Wales. His transformation to centre-half, as already discussed, took place by accident following an injury to regular pivot Billy Smith. By the end of the 1960-61 season Ure had played in 32 games, most at centre-half, and the following year he was ever present. Ure would make a total of 133 appearances in five years but, curiously, never scored. Considering his height, it is surprising that he did not present a greater threat from corner-kicks or set-pieces. Ure says he lost interest in taking penalties when, aged twelve, he took a kick for his school team, Newtonpark: 'As skipper I cockily decided to nominate myself to take it and shot high over the bar and although we won in extra time I had no interest in ever taking another penalty unless the rest of the team fell down in a fit.'

Ure won eleven full caps, eight as a Dundee player. By the time he collected his Player of the Year award his team were struggling in the league, but were through to the third round of the Scottish Cup, courtesy of huge wins over Inverness Caledonian and Montrose.

Having lost four years earlier to Fraserburgh, nothing was taken for granted in icy Inverness. Shankly was concerned that the players' anxiety was disrupting their preparations, so decided to take matters into his own hands. Without telling anyone, Shankly and trainer Sammy Kean sneaked out of the team hotel at 10pm to see if they could inspect the pitch.

Needless to say, at that time of night Telford Park was locked up, so they climbed over the wall. They found the pitch cleared of snow, as Caley were keen for the game to go ahead with a bumper all-ticket capacity crowd expected. In view of the rock-hard pitch, Shankly duly procured a set of rubber boots for his players and Dundee won 5-1. At home to Montrose, they then scored eight.

The worst winter in memory wiped out all Dundee's league fixtures, so that, by the the time they took the field in Anderlecht on 6 March, those two one-sided Scottish Cup-ties constituted their only competitive outings in two months.

On paper, Anderlecht appeared formidable opponents. This was their fourth appearance in the European Cup, but the first time they had reached the last eight. They had won the Belgian league nine times since the War and, in their mauve and white strip, they used a 4-2-4 style with an emphasis on attack. Facing nine internationalists in the Belgian line up, Dundee were given little chance of reaching the semis.

Paul Van Himst, aged nineteen, is remembered by Gilzean and Ure as the danger man. Van Himst was the current Belgian Player of the Year and had already been capped sixteen times.

Interest in the tie was so huge that Anderlecht moved the game from their own ground in Brussels to the national Heysel Stadium elsewhere in the city, which could hold 60,000. Among that number were some 200 Dundee supporters who had made their way to Belgium by plane, train and car. Dickson's Travel Office in Reform Street ran two 'Continental Football Specials'. The first bus left Dundee on the Monday. The fare, including travel, two nights in a Brussels hotel, main meals and match tickets was £17 10s. The second, leaving on Tuesday with only one night in Brussels, cost £15. Both buses were full.

One supporter who left on the first bus was Ian Smith of Inchture, just outside Dundee, who left home without his passport. Realising his mistake, at Dover he was driven to the Ministry of Labour to apply for a new one. Armed with a new photograph, Ian soon had a new passport in his hands and boarded the ferry with five minutes to spare.

The official party flew to Brussels direct from Turnhouse and took the field in front of a full house. Their Belgian hosts played 'The Dundee Song' by Hector Nicol. The Dundee fans present sung along with gusto, but were perplexed when it was followed by the 'Tannadice Song'. Having had both records sent over, Anderlecht secretary Eugene Steppe wasn't sure which one to play, so played both!

The game kicked off and – with the Belgian TV cameraman caught napping – Dundee promptly scored. A sight of Gilzean's quick-fire goal from Gordon Smith's cross was therefore denied to those outside the stadium. Happily, the cameraman had Gilzean in his sights when he fired in from outside the box to make it 2-0 and take his personal European tally to eight.

Back home, Patrick Barclay remembers listening to the game on his radio by picking up a Belgian station. Even though the commentary was in Flemish, he soon got the gist as, 'every time Gilzean was mentioned a groan followed'.

The game ended 4-1 to Dundee and once again the result sent shockwaves through Europe. 'Those European nights were very special,' says Gilzean, 'and that performance in Anderlecht was very special indeed. We had played some great stuff and the Belgians knew they had witnessed a fantastic performance from Dundee and at the end of the game the Belgian crowd gave us a standing ovation and clapped us off the pitch.'

It wasn't just the Anderlecht fans who knew they had seen something special, but the Anderlecht players too. At the post-match reception each Dundee player was presented with a cigar box and a silver cigarette lighter. The Belgians even provided an extra six to take back for those players who hadn't travelled.

The Anderlecht coach, Pierre Sinibaldi, acknowledged Dundee's fine performance, while Shankly said: 'It was a clash of styles and Anderlecht lost because they couldn't change their tactics. Before the match we would have settled for a draw, but we took our chances and, after all, that's football.' Proud Dundee chairman James Gellatly said he was 'completely overcome and never expected such a fine a win as this'. Back in Dundee, fans eager for news of the result flooded the switchboard at the *Courier* from 6.45pm onwards. By 8.30 the operator couldn't cope with the volume of calls coming in.

As the news spread throughout the city, there was many a celebration 'hauf' in the public houses. In the Silver Tassie in Lochee, mine host Ed Summerton gave free nips all round, while in the Volunteer Arms in Bell Street Dundee fans were joined by members of the Territorial Army who went out to celebrate when they heard the score.

Bobby Cox described that night in Brussels as 'Dundee at their very best. We took everything they threw at us and when they gave us space we were lethal. It was a proud night for all of us.'

With the second leg at Dens a week later a seeming formality, just 89 Anderlecht supporters made the journey across to Scotland. For Dundee fans, European Cup fever swept through the city. Tickets were at a premium as 40,000 supporters snapped up briefs for a crowd that exceeded even that which had watched Cologne and Sporting Lisbon.

With nothing to lose, Anderlecht dictated play and drew first blood after half an hour. Gilzean was not at his sharpest, but he'd had six stitches for an ankle cut in Brussels and had missed the weekend's 0-1 defeat by Airdrie. He had the stitches removed in order to play, and his very presence ensured that he was marshalled by two Anderlecht defenders throughout the match. Two Dundee goals in the closing minutes ensured an outcome that had never been seriously tested and allowed the team the satisfaction of winning both legs.

Things were shaping up nicely. Five days later, Gilzean's header enabled Dundee to knock Hibs out of the Scottish Cup and book a place in the quarter-finals for the first time in eleven years. The draw now brought Rangers to Dens Park, and another huge crowd – 37,000 – braved a soaking to witness a thriller which ended 1-1. It might have been worse, as Rangers had the ball in the net in the final minute but the referee, after consulting his linesman, chalked it off.

The replay, four days later, saw the gates closed on a crowd of 82,000, the biggest attendance to see any Dundee game since the Scottish Cup final of 1952. Dundee hadn't lost a league game in Govan for six years and went into the match in confident mood, even though Rangers were unbeaten at home this season in which they romped to the championship. The match tilted one way then the other. Alex Hamilton's own-goal was erased by two Gilzean goals either side of half-time. Poor Hamilton then obstructed Wilson and Brand put away the penalty. Two minutes from time Brand got his second to send Dundee out of the cup.

In the league, Dundee were not acquitting themselves well. Successive defeats by Celtic, Queen of the South, and Hibs, left the press suggesting that the Dark Blues were saving their energies for the European Cup. Gordon Smith denied this, claiming that 'Dundee were now the team everyone wanted to beat,' but the Dundee *Sporting Post* suggested that the team needed to vary their tactics.

With the severe winter wiping out most of January and February, Dundee were now playing at least two games a week to catch up, and the backlog was beginning to take its toll on some of the older players. Bob Shankly seemed reluctant to alter his strongest team and Bobby Wishart feels that everyone might have benefited if Gordon Smith, now 39, Bobby Seith and himself, both 32, had been rested during this punishing schedule.

All eyes, however, were now on the European Cup semi-final draw. The other three clubs involved were Benfica, AC Milan and Feyenoord. Feyenoord appeared to be the weakest and therefore most desirable opponents, as Benfica were defending the Cup and AC Milan – who had beaten English champions Ipswich Town in an earlier round – were now the favourites. As Dundee had already beaten one Portuguese team, the opponents they desperately wanted to avoid were Milan.

With the final scheduled for Wembley, Ian Ure felt that if Dundee could surmount this last obstacle they would go on to lift the trophy. 'It would have seemed like a home tie for Dundee and so I doubt any side would have beaten us at Wembley.' Ure and Alex Hamilton had already played at Wembley that season as part of the Scottish side that defeated the English 2-1. Both Dundee players loved the experience and were eager to return with their club.

As luck would have it, Dundee were paired with Milan. By this time Dundee were attracting much media interest inside Scotland and overseas, and the club was featured in the press, on radio, and on TV, most notably on BBC's midweek Sportsview with Peter Dimmock.

In the *Courier* an unnamed female reporter interviewed the players' wives on their home life and how their husbands prepared for a big game. Betty Cox said: 'Bobby doesn't sleep too well the night before the match and he likes to go to bed a little bit earlier than usual. His appetite isn't really affected. He has a light lunch with the team just before the match but, at other times, he eats a lot. When the match is over, the tension relaxes a bit and the night after the game Bobby likes to get down to all his odd jobs.' Alex Hamilton's wife, Norah, claimed that her husband was neither up nor down before or after a match and he sleeps like he always does – 'restless'. 'Alex may worry a bit when he is actually at Dens or wherever he happens to be playing, but he never shows pre-match nerves at home and his appetite is never affected.'

In the run up to the semi, Dundee's erratic league form continued. A 5-1 home win over St Mirren was followed by defeats to Dundee United at home (0-1) and Motherwell away (1-2). The loss to United was particularly sore as it was their rivals' first ever league win at Dens. It was hardly the best preparation for the biggest game of the players' lives.

The build up was a source of anger for supporters, who complained bitterly about the hike in ticket prices for the second leg at home. While the normal admission price was three shillings (15p), the prices for the Milan game were set at £2 for the centre stand, £1 10s for the wing stands, twelve shillings and sixpence (67½p) for the enclosure and seven shilling and sixpence (37½p) for admission to the ground.

Two days before the team flew out to Milan, captain Bobby Cox tore a cartilage and was ruled out. Nevertheless, the party was in high spirits and a Lion Rampart was unfurled for the waiting media when the players disembarked.

Milan had nine internationalists in their ranks. Among them were Giovanni Trappatoni, captain Cesare Maldini, and golden boy Gianni Rivera. The kick-off was delayed to allow 78,000 spectators to pack the San Siro, and within three minutes Milan were ahead when Sani nodded home. When Cousin headed in Penman's cross, Dundee briefly had their tails up. They were still on level terms at half-time, but problems were mounting. Bert Slater was being blinded by a battery of camera flashes every time he went for the ball. Shankly complained about this to the Italian officials and to Spanish referee Caballero, but to no avail. Indeed, the referee, according to Tommy Gallacher in the *Courier*, showed such bias that 'every time a Dundee player went near their Italian counterparts he made it impossible for Dundee to tackle them'.

Dundee, on the other hand, were being subjected to some fierce tackling and Gordon Smith and Alan Gilzean in particular were coming in for rough treatment. Gilzean recalls how the Peruvian defender, Victor Benitez, singled him out, pursuing him about the park, continually pulling his jersey, kicking him and spitting on him. 'They were such a class side and didn't need such tactics and their tactics were diabolical. We really saw the highs and lows of European football in that run.'

Indeed, some weeks after the tie in Milan, suspicions that Dundee had been dealt unfairly in the San Siro by the referee were given credence when the official was found to have accepted extravagant gifts from the Italian club during another game, and was banned from officiating pending charges of bribery.

In spite of everything, it was still 1-1 with everything to play for in the second half. Ian Ure remembers how the players started thinking about the final and how close they now were to Wembley. It took away the focus on the job they still had to do in the second half. Dundee's dream of being the first British club to reach the European Cup final took a terrible dunt as Milan scored two quick goals. Both were controversial. The ball appeared to have gone out of play before one goal, and a Milan player was standing on the goal-line offside for the second. Indeed, the linesman raised his flag, but was overruled.

In the closing minutes Dundee were stunned by further goals from Milan's wingers, Barison and Mora. Milan cleverly drew Ure out of position before hitting high balls to the near post, where Barison easily outjumped Hamilton. 'It was clinical finishing from Milan, which the defenders could do little about,' says Ure. 'Near-post flashing headers with quick players nipping in and we allowed ourselves to be forced back a bit. And after such a great start, the tie was gone.' All five Milan goals had come from high crosses, against which Dundee were usually well-prepared.

Despite the fact that in the second leg Dundee were playing only for pride, 38,000 still turned up at Dens. Bob Shankly fielded an unchanged side. Milan defended in depth and broke up Dundee's rhythm at every opportunity. Gilzean did convert a Smith cross to put the Dees ahead on the night, and thereafter Dundee squealed for penalties whenever a player went down. Smith and Gilzean took terrible punishment, and when Gillie sought retribution he was sent off for lashing out at Benitez. 'I am not proud of it,' says Gillie, 'but I had just about had enough and just lashed out without thinking.'

It was a sad end to Dundee's European Cup adventure. Tommy Gallacher described it as 'one of the most bruising and bitter battles ever seen at Dens Park, where flailing boots and raised fists were commonplace.'

In total, Dundee played eight games in their European campaign, winning five and losing three. Had they posted such results in the modern-day Champions League format, they would surely have qualified from their group. Ian Ure says he prefers the old Champions Cup format to the current one, when only national champions were entered and it was played on a knock-out basis from start to finish.

Milan went on to lift the trophy, defeating Benfica 2-1 at Wembley. In *Dundee Greats*, Alex Hamilton tells the author, Jim Hendry, that he felt after watching the final that Dundee 'playing badly could have beaten the pair of them'. It was the first time AC Milan, or indeed any Italian club, had lifted the European Cup.

For Dundee the European adventure was over and the domestic campaign limped to its undistinguished conclusion. Ironically the last game of the season saw Dundee meet the newly crowned Champions of Scotland Rangers, the game ending goalless. In defending their title Dundee finished a disappointing ninth, losing more games than they won. And that meant no more European football.

Chapter 8

~ How The Mighty Fell ~

(1963 – 1976)

'You can sing of the glories of teams you have seen,
Of the Saints or the Dons up in Old Aberdeen,
But in all this wide world, there's but one team for me,
It's the bold boys who wear the Dark Blue o' Dundee.

Let the proud Rangers sing of the records they hold,
Let Celtic acclaim all their heroes of old,
We will follow and follow o'er land and o'er sea,
For the brave boys who wear the Dark Blue o' Dundee.

Oh there's many a battle been fought on this field,
And there's many teams learnt that Dundee never yield,
For although on occasion, defeat we must know,
We will rise up again and we'll beat every foe.

Oh there's Robertson, Penman and Alan Gilzean,
With Cousin and Smith, they're the finest you've seen,
A defence that is steady, heroic and sure,
Liney, Hamilton, Cox, Seith and Wishart and Ure.'

The Dundee Song: Hector Nicol 1962
(Traditional Scots tune *Bonnie Dundee*)

The Dundee Championship side and their European adventures are the stuff of legend but their fall from grace is a salutary tale which has plagued so many provincial clubs who have reached the heights and dreams that exceeded their stature.

But fate had allowed Dundee to live their dreams and brought together a bunch of players who would blend both on and off the park into what Dave Webster describes on the 'Dundee Mad' website as 'the complete dream team'. 'To have so many of different abilities,' Dave writes, 'to arrive at exactly the same time is what made this team so special.' There were young stars like Alan Gilzean, who had trained as a painter and decorator, Ian Ure, who had given up rugby to play football for Dundee, and Andy Penman, the homesick genius whom Willie Thornton had rescued from Everton at the tender age of fifteen.

There was the ageing genius, Gordon Smith, who had been put out to pasture by Hearts with four championship medals in his pocket, whom Bob Shankly picked up for nothing at the age of 37 and would play in a European Cup semi-final at 39. There were fellow veterans Bobby Wishart and Bobby Seith who had championships behind them with Aberdeen and Burnley respectively, who would bring vital experience to a young team.

There was Alan Cousin, a part-time footballer who juggled his playing career with school teaching and whose double shuffle was something that could never be taught. There was Hugh Robertson, deft and electric on the left wing, and goalkeeper Pat Liney, without whom the championship might not have been won if he hadn't saved that penalty against St Mirren in the penultimate game.

There was Alex Hamilton, a joker and an extrovert, whose party-piece was playing keepie-up with a sixpence before flicking it up and catching it in his pocket, and fellow full-back Bobby Cox who, with his famous sliding tackle, captained the club he loved to the Scottish title. They all combined to make Dundee the Champions of Scotland, whether by divine intervention, destiny, hard work, or good luck, or perhaps just a little of all of them.

After winning the Scottish League title, however, Dundee never finished higher than fifth, and just fourteen years later were relegated to the Scottish League's second tier. With hindsight, finishing in the top ten was achievement in itself. In the seasons immediately before and after lifting the title, Dundee finished tenth and ninth. On both occasions the Dees would have been relegated from a top-ten elite, exactly what came to pass when that elite materialised as the Premier League in 1975. They finished ninth on another two occasions after 1963, prior to the Premier League's introduction, so their right to a place among the elite can hardly be taken for granted. True, in 1964 Dundee reached the Scottish Cup final, but it would be the last time they did for 39 years.

Two years after winning the league, most of the side remained intact. Eight of the players who collected loser's medals at Hampden in 1964 had championship medals from 1962. But by then the side had already started to break up.

In May 1963, in the wake of elimination by AC Milan, Alex Hamilton and Ian Ure put in transfer requests, and Alan Gilzean dallied over a new contract. According to Jim Wilkie's *Across The Great Divide*, 'it had been known since the late fifties that the future of the British football teams in terms of earning power and prestige lay in the European competitions and these games also served to give players some idea of their individual standing in the international game.' With Dundee now having made their mark, several players felt that a move away would benefit their career and their bank balance.

Dundee's championship came near the end of one of the most competitive eras in Scottish football. Since 1945, twelve different clubs had lifted a major trophy (Rangers, Celtic, Aberdeen, Motherwell, Clyde, Dunfermline, St Mirren, Falkirk, East Fife, Hearts, Hibs and Dundee) and Bobby Wishart refers to this time as 'the Golden era of Scottish football'. He points out that it wasn't really until the mid-1960s, when players started to move down south in big transfers, that provincial clubs could no longer hold on to their best players. Hitherto, with a maximum wage in operation, players had no monetary incentive to migrate to big-city clubs. They generally only moved when they were superfluous to requirements. Players therefore were happy enough to stay where they were, provided they were successful.

Attendances in the 1950s were also much higher than in the following decades. The gate money coming in meant that clubs didn't have to sell to survive. When attendances began to drop, clubs began to look towards transfer fees for income and for provincial clubs players suddenly became saleable assets. Added to this, the maximum wage had been abolished in England, whose clubs could now tempt players from Scotland. Dressing room gossip whenever players gathered for internationals fuelled the trend. A generation of 'Anglo-Scots' was about to be born.

At Dens, Alex Hamilton had struggled in Scotland's tour of Norway and the Republic of Ireland and was dropped for the final match with Spain. Frustrated by his lack of international progress, he initially thought he would benefit from a move. He soon changed his mind, however, as being a contract rebel might harm his international career even more. Hamilton re-signed, and so in the end did Alan Gilzean.

Ian Ure, however, vowed never to kick another ball for Dundee. Such was his determination to leave that, when the club stopped his wages in June, he intended to seek unemployment benefit of £3 7s 6d a week rather than back down. Instead, Ure was offered a sales job by washing machine tycoon John Bloom, who happened to be an Arsenal fan. When Dundee finally agreed to listen to offers for Ure, it was no surprise that the Gunners were first in the queue.

Ure had already impressed against Arsenal in two friendlies, and Highbury boss Billy Wright tempted Dundee with a world record fee for a centre-half of £62,500. Dundee could hardly say no, for it was also the largest fee ever offered for a player in Scotland. Bob Shankly said later that he was offered the keys to a £5,000 Bentley by an unnamed English club if Ure could be 'steered in the right direction'.

Ure's final appearance for Dundee was on 5 May 1963 in the last game of the season when he helped his side keep a clean sheet in a 0-0 draw with new champions Rangers.

Season 1963-64 was a transitional one for the Dark Blues. In February, 40-year-old Gordon Smith, at his own request, was allowed to leave. His last game for the club was on New Year's Day 1964, a 1-4 home defeat by Aberdeen. After retiring from the game, he opened a pub, aptly named 'The Right Wing', and according to John Cairney's *A Scottish Football Hall of Fame,* 'the game is not the same without him'.

Smith was therefore absent from the side which lost the 1964 Scottish Cup final to Rangers. George McGeachie and Pat Liney had also departed. The previous season McGeachie had started work as an industrial chemist in Teesside after a dispute with the club. As for Liney, after claiming his championship medal he played only twice more for the Dark Blues. Early in 1964 he joined St Mirren, the team he had supported as a boy, for £4,000. After two years at Love Street he moved to Bradford Park Avenue, then neighbours Bradford City, where in later years he provided 'hospitality' on matchdays.

Nor was there a place in the 1964 final for Bobby Wishart, who featured only four times that season. The following August, now aged 34, Wishart joined Airdrie on a free transfer, leaving behind a Dundee career of 95 appearances and ten goals.

In the aftermath of the Hampden defeat, Gilzean made up his mind to cash in on his worth. Season 1963-64 had seen him score an incredible 52 club goals in all competitions, plus three for Scotland. While on international duty, Gilzean shared a room with Spurs' John White, who talked of earning a fortune. At that time there were no long-term contacts and players had to sign on every year, but this time Gilzean refused.

'Nowadays there are commercial earnings and sponsorship,' says Gilzean, 'but then the only income the clubs could rely on was the gate receipts and it meant that it came to the stage where Bob Shankly couldn't offer us any more. I was also concerned that, as an internationalist, my position in the Scotland team might be affected if I stayed at Dens as they weren't a club who won something every year.'

By the time the 1964-65 season kicked-off, Dundee were still refusing to sell their star striker. He was in contractual limbo, unable to kick a football until he signed for someone. By October, Dundee, still holding his registration, agreed a two-month contract, and in Gilzean's first game back he scored two goals at St Mirren. The player was not, however, eligible for Dundee's return to Europe, as he had re-signed after that season's deadline, so he missed out on Dundee's tie with Real Zaragoza in the Cup-Winner's Cup. The tie finished 4-3 to the Spanish side on aggregate and Dundee's return to Europe was brief.

When Gilzean did go, to Tottenham for £72,500, his fee even exceeded the previous Scottish record for Ian Ure. Gillie signed off his Dundee career with a headed hat trick in a 4-4 draw with St Johnstone on 5 December 1964. He left as Dundee's all-time record goalscorer with 165 goals in his seven years at Dens, and record scorer for one season with 52 goals in 1963-64. Both records still stand.

Three months after Gilzean, the Dens Park faithful suffered another blow when the mastermind of their greatest hour, Bob Shankly, also left. He had been disillusioned at Dens for some time, and had deferred signing a new contract that had been on the table since the previous season. Gilzean's sale was the final straw. Craig Brown remembers that early in 1965 Falkirk made an approach for him. Brown sought Shankly's advice and was told: 'Son, I'm getting out of here and I would advise you to do the same!' Bob had already turned down an offer from Kilmarnock, was thought to have been tempted by Rangers, but in March 1965 quit to take over Hibs, whose manager, Jock Stein, had left to take charge at Celtic.

Bob Shankly died in 1982. He was then general manager at Stirling Albion – which had caused wry amusement. For a while, two Shankly brothers, Bill and Bob, had been in charge at An(n)field. Bob Shankly will never be forgotten at Dens Park. In 1999 the fans voted to name one of the new stands the 'Bob Shankly Stand'.

Days before Bob passed away, another Dundee legend, Billy Steel, also died. At the next home game, against Airdrie, a minute's silence was held for both. Dundee won the match 1-0 to avoid relegation.

Before leaving Dens for Easter Road, Shankly sold another two of the championship side. Bobby Waddell went to Blackpool for £10,000 and Craig Brown to Falkirk for £6,000. Waddell in total made 79 appearances for Dundee, scoring 43 times, though his only goal in the championship year was the vital one that beat Hibs in March. Craig Brown was the first player Shankly signed for Dundee and the last he sold. Brown was soon forced to quit the game through injury, but went on to make his name as a successful manager of the Scotland national team.

Curiously, of the fifteen players who won a championship medal with Dundee, only two, Craig Brown and Bobby Seith, made any real impact as a manager. Seith played at Dens for five seasons. His swansong came at the site of Dundee's greatest triumph, when after 193 appearances for the club, he bowed out in a 0-1 defeat at Muirton Park in February 1965. Seith, who held coaching certificates from the English and Scottish FAs, joined the coaching staff at Dens under Shankly's replacement, Bobby Ancell. In later years he served Rangers, Preston and Hearts, before setting up a chiropody practice in Dundee.

In May 1965, Sammy Kean left to become manager of Falkirk and, when physiotherapist Lawrie Smith also departed, it marked the end of the successful Shankly-Kean-Smith backroom team. Kean had become caretaker manager at Dens following the departure of Shankly and in his six games in charge Dundee won two, drew three and lost one before he moved to take the Brockville job.

On the playing side, Hugh Robertson was sold in May to Dunfermline for £13,000. He later played and coached at Arbroath, returned to Dens as youth coach and chief scout, and after a spell in Denmark returned to this country where he now runs a pub in Ayrshire. During his Dark Blue playing career, Hugh chalked up 287 appearances for the club, notching 61 goals in the process. He also gained one full international cap.

Bert Slater was also released, but returned to Dens in 1987 as youth coach and chief scout, a position he held under managers Jocky Scott, Dave Smith and Gordon Wallace. Alex Hamilton was appointed club captain but in November 1965 Alan Cousin rejoined Bob Shankly at Hibs for a fee of £15,500. Cousin had been voted Dundee Player of the Year five months previously but, with the arrival of Charlie Cooke from Aberdeen, the big schoolteacher was surplus to requirements. Cousin left behind him a legacy of 141 goals in 379 appearances. Perhaps the most remarkable fact about the man renowned for his double shuffle was that throughout his footballing career he stayed part-time. After retiring, he taught in his native Clackmannanshire, where he still stays.

At the start of 1965-66, Hamilton and Penman received large signing-on fees after agreeing long-term deals, but a year later both were put up for sale after repeated transfer requests. The loss of Penman was hard to take, but when he threatened to do a 'Billy Steel' and join a new rebel US league, the club faced losing out on a transfer fee. In April the £55,000-rated star joined Rangers in exchange for George McLean and £30,000.

Penman had missed only two games in Dundee's championship season and was an ever present the following year during the European Cup campaign. In total he played 287 games for Dundee, scoring 129 goals. Surprisingly, given that he signed for one of the Old Firm, his Dundee champions medal was the only winners' medal he ever earned. He later played for Arbroath and Highland League side Inverness Caledonian.

Andy Penman died in 1994, aged just 51, but his legacy lives on. One of the hospitality lounges at Dens Park is named after him, and on entering the main door of the stadium, a picture of Andy greets visitors in the foyer with the simple caption 'the Penalty King'.

By the time Penman left, another member of the championship side had played his last game. Alex Hamilton made his last appearance in Dark Blue in February 1967 in a 3-5 defeat at Motherwell. That brought down the curtain on 338 appearances, and he was eventually freed in August 1968. With 24 full Scottish caps, he remains the club's record cap holder and in fact Hamilton earned 34 caps at all levels. He and his family emigrated to South Africa before returning to Dundee in 1990, charming a new generation of Dundee supporters as he entertained guests in the Dens Park Executive Club. Hamilton died in July 1993. The club duly renamed one of its hospitality lounges the 'Alex Hamilton Lounge'.

Season 1967-68 saw only two of the championship side left at Dens. In October, Dundee reached the League Cup final, where they lost 3-5 to Celtic. Alec Stuart was in the starting eleven and Bobby Cox on the bench. Dundee also reached the Fairs Cup semi-final that season and both players helped take them there. Leeds United denied Dundee a place in the final. 1968-69 marked Cox's last season for Dundee when he played just twice in the League Cup in August. The following summer, aged 35, and after thirteen years at Dens Park, Cox was released, alongside Stuart, who made his final appearance on 4 January 1969. Stuart thereby became the last of the championship team to play for Dundee.

Sadly, the club did not build on their title success, despite profiting by £250,000 in transfer fees alone. According to Jim Wilkie's *Across The Great Divide*, this was 'a sum of money which should have enabled them to mount a sustained and effective challenge for honours in Scotland and Europe.' It didn't.

As the championship team was sold off, the club failed to establish a scouting system to equal that which had unearthed the likes of Gilzean, Ure, Hamilton and Cox. Dundee would pay the price of this lack of foresight for the next 40 years.

The exploits of the 1961-62 championship side will never be forgotten. Skipper Bobby Cox still remains at Dens, working in the Captains Lounge on matchdays, a revered figure. On Dundee's return to Europe after a 29-year absence in August 2003, 'Sir Robert' accompanied the official party to Albania. His presence around Dens Park is a visible and constant reminder of the Champions of Scotland.

GUIDE TO SEASONAL SUMMARIES

Col 1: Match number (for league fixtures); Round (for cup-ties).
e.g. 4R means 'Fourth round replay.'

Col 2: Date of the fixture and whether Home (H), Away (A), or Neutral (N).

Col 3: Opposition.

Col 4: Attendances. Home gates appear in roman; Away gates in *italics.*
Figures in **bold** indicate the largest and smallest gates, at home and away.
Average home and away attendances appear after the final league match.

Col 5: Respective league positions of Dundee and opponents after the game.
Dundee's position appears on the top line in roman.
Their opponents' position appears on the second line in *italics.*
For cup-ties, the division and position of opponents is provided.
e.g. 2:12 means the opposition are twelfth in Division 2.

Col 6: The top line shows the result: W(in), D(raw), or L(ose).
The second line shows Dundee's cumulative points total.

Col 7: The match score, Dundee's given first.
Scores in **bold** show Dundee's biggest league win and heaviest defeat.

Col 8: The half-time score, Dundee's given first.

Col 9: The top line shows Dundee's scorers and times of goals in roman.
The second line shows opponents' scorers and times of goals in *italics.*
A 'p' after the time of a goal denotes a penalty; 'og' an own-goal.
The third line gives the name of the match referee.

Team line-ups: Dundee line-ups appear on top line, irrespective of whether
they are home or away. Opposition teams are on the second line in *italics.*
Players of either side who are sent off are marked !
Dundee players making their league debuts are displayed in **bold**.

No	Date		Att	Pos	Pt	F-A	H-T	Scorers, Times, and Referees	1	2	3	4	5	6	7	8	9	10	11
1	A	FALKIRK			W	3-1	2-0	Smith 5, Cousin 37, Wishart 71	Liney	Hamilton	Cox	Seith	Ure	Wishart	**Smith**	Penman	Gilzean	Cousin	Robertson
	23/8		*7,000*		2			*Wyles 90*	*Whigham*	*Rae*	*Hunter*	*McCarry*	*Milne*	*McIntosh*	*Wyles*	*Murray*	*Lambie*	*Reid*	*Ormond*
								Ref: A McKenzie (Coatbridge)	Smith gets his first Dundee league goal against Shankly's former club when he nets a Penman pass, which Gilzean had dummied. Two Smith crosses let Cousin and Wishart score with their heads. With no floodlights on, Wyles scores past an unsighted Liney in the midweek darkness.										
2	H	DUNDEE UTD		2	W	4-1	3-1	Penman 11, Smith 13, Briggs 32 (og)	Liney	Hamilton	Cox	Seith	Ure	Stuart	Smith	Penman	Gilzean	Cousin	Robertson
	9/9		20,000	*12*	4			*Gillespie 34* [Robertson 83]	*Ugolini*	*Graham*	*Briggs*	*Neilson*	*Smith*	*Fraser*	*Carlyle*	*Gillespie*	*Mochan*	*Irvine*	*McDonald*
								Ref: J Stewart (Paisley)	Dundee have still never lost to Utd at Dens in the league. Former Utd player Davie Dorward flies in from Canada especially to see the match but witnesses left-back Jimmy Briggs run a Robertson shot past his own keeper. Dundee move into second place in the league behind Rangers.										
3	A	ABERDEEN		6	L	1-3	0-2	Gilzean 66	Liney	Hamilton	Cox	Seith	Ure	Stuart	Smith	Penman	Gilzean	Cousin	Robertson
	16/9		*12,000*	*3*	4			*Kinnell 23p, Brownlee 45, Little 51*	*Ogston*	*Cadenhead*	*Hogg*	*Barry*	*Kinnell*	*Fraser*	*Baird*	*Brownlee*	*Little*	*Cooke*	*Thom*
								Ref: A Crossman (Edinburgh)	A penalty is given when Hamilton is adjudged to have handled the ball as he stoops to head away a Charlie Cooke cross. A hopeful roar comes from the Dons support and the ref, wearing an eye shield and despite being yards from the incident, consults his linesman who awards the kick.										
4	H	HEARTS		2	W	2-0	1-0	Gilzean 31, 71	Liney	Hamilton	Cox	Seith	Ure	Wishart	Smith	Penman	Cousin	Gilzean	Robertson
	23/9		12,000	*14*	6				*Marshall*	*Kirk*	*Holt*	*Ferguson*	*Polland*	*Cumming*	*Wallace*	*Hamilton*	*Paton*	*Higgins*	*Blackwood*
								Ref: D Minto (Hurlford)	Dundee line up in the white change kit to avoid a clash with the Jambos' maroon. A short back-pass from Tynecastle captain John Cumming is intercepted by Penman who squares to Gilzean for a tap in. Gillie's second double of the season comes from his head after a Robertson cross.										
5	A	THIRD LANARK		2	W	3-1	1-0	Gilzean 25, 84, Cousin 60	Liney	Hamilton	Cox	Seith	Ure	Wishart	Smith	Penman	Cousin	Gilzean	Robertson
	30/9		*9,500*	*11*	8			*McInnes 78*	*Robertson*	*McGillvray*	*Lewis*	*Reilly*	*McCormack*	*Cunningham*	*Goodfellow*	*Hilley*	*Harley*	*Gray*	*McInnes*
								Ref: W Fyfe (Edinburgh)	Dundee's first win in three matches against the George Young's side this season, shows their championship potential with a comfortable win. Hi-Hi's keeper Jocky Robertson is inspired but can't stop two Gilzean goals from Seith crosses, or a Cousin strike from the corner of the box.										
6	H	KILMARNOCK		1	W	5-3	2-2	W'son 34 (og), P'man 36, 59, 80, Gilz'n 54	Liney	Hamilton	Cox	Seith	Ure	Wishart	Smith	Penman	Cousin	Gilzean	Robertson
	7/10		14,000	*4*	10			*McInally 2, McIlroy 45, Watson 87*	*McLaughlin*	*Richmond*	*Watson*	*Davidson*	*McGrory*	*Beattie*	*McIlroy*	*Mason*	*Black*	*McInally*	*Mair*
								Ref: W Elliot (Barrhead)	Dundee move to the top of the table for the first as Rangers are inactive due to international commitments. Penman broke an ankle against Killie last season but got revenge with his second hat-trick for Dundee. Watson glanced a header past his own keeper from a Robertson corner.										
7	A	MOTHERWELL		1	W	4-2	2-1	Penman 1p, Cousin 28, Smith 71,	Liney	Hamilton	Cox	Seith	Ure	Wishart	Smith	Penman	Cousin	Gilzean	Robertson
	14/10		*15,000*	*5*	12			*Hunter 25, Roberts 70* [Gilzean 76]	*Weir*	*McSeveney*	*Thomson*	*Aitken*	*Martis*	*McCann*	*Lindsay*	*Quinn*	*Roberts*	*Hunter*	*Stevenson*
								Ref: J Paterson (Linlithgow)	With release of Doug Cowie, whose 445 appearances for Dundee is an all-time record, in the summer, Andy Penman has now taken on the role of penalty taker. An Aitken handball gives Andy his first league penalty for Dundee with The Dees now having averaged three goals per game.										
8	A	DUNFERMLINE		1	W	2-1	0-1	Cousin 57, 82	Liney	Hamilton	Cox	Seith	Ure	Wishart	Smith	Penman	Cousin	Gilzean	Robertson
	21/10		*10,000*	*12*	14			*Mailer 25p*	*Connachan*	*Fraser*	*Cunningham*	*Mailer*	*Williamson*	*Miller*	*McDonald*	*Peebles*	*D Smith*	*A Smith*	*Melrose*
								Ref: D Alexander (Edinburgh)	Jock Stein's men are going well in Europe and a Hamilton foul on Melrose allows Mailer score from the spot. Dundee effectively play with ten men after Smith is injured in the first minute, though he completes the game. Cousin's winner sends the keeper the wrong way with his head.										
9	H	PARTICK TH		1	W	3-2	1-1	Cousin 30, 88, Penman 68p,	Liney	Hamilton	Cox	Seith	Ure	Wishart	McGeachie	Penman	Cousin	Gilzean	Robertson
	28/10		16,000	*6*	16			*McParland 10, Cunningham 82*	*Gray*	*Hogan*	*Brown*	*Cunningham*	*McKinnon*	*Dunlevy*	*Williamson*	*McBride*	*Smith*	*Duffy*	*McParland*
								Ref: J Mackie (East Kilbride)	Dundee extend their lead to five points with Rangers playing in the League Cup final v Hearts at Hampden. Gilzean has an early goal chopped for offside. The Jags equalise from a free-kick which is chipped over wall to Cunningham, ignoring manager Willie Waddell's shouts to shoot.										
10	H	CELTIC		1	W	2-1	1-1	Wishart 8, Gilzean 59	Liney	Hamilton	Cox	Seith	Ure	Wishart	Smith	Penman	Cousin	Gilzean	Robertson
	4/11		24,500	*4*	18			*Carroll 21*	*Haffey*	*McKay*	*Kennedy*	*Crerand*	*McNamee*	*Clark*	*Chalmers*	*Jackson*	*Hughes*	*Divers*	*Carroll*
								Ref: W Mullen (Cardenden)	Crowd trouble breaks out at both the game and town centre where many pubs are closed early on the orders of the police. Wishart is given time and space to score from 20 yards. Jimmy McGrory's Bhoys equalise when Carroll shows a fine turn of speed before Gilzean nods the winner.										
11	A	RANGERS		1	W	**5-1**	0-0	Gilzean 47, 48, 74, 87, Penman 88	Liney	Hamilton	Cox	Seith	Ure	Wishart	Smith	Penman	Cousin	Gilzean	Robertson
	11/11		*38,000*	*3*	20			*Brand 84*	*Ritchie*	*Shearer*	*Caldow*	*Davis*	*Paterson*	*Baxter*	*Scott*	*McMillan*	*Christie*	*Brand*	*Wilson*
								Ref: R Rodger (Stonehouse)	Swirling fog makes visibility very poor and police turn back many Dundee buses, saying that the game is off. Those that get in are unsure how many Dundee score in the second half. Penman moves to man mark Baxter at half-time. Scot Symon's men can't cope with Gilzean in the air.										

12	H	RAITH		1	W	5-4	0-1	Gilz' 50, 52, Wish' 69, Seith 86, Smith 87	Liney	Hamilton	Cox	Seith	Ure	Wishart	Smith	Penman	Cousin	Gilzean	Robertson
	18/11		15,000	*17*	22			*Leigh 22, Clinton 58, Lourie 60, Adam'n 6*	*Cunningham*	*Wilson*	*Mochan*	*Stein*	*Forysth*	*Leigh*	*Lourie*	*White*	*Adamson*	*Clinton*	*Watson*
								Ref: E Cowan (Glasgow)	Dundee gain revenge over the Kirkcaldy side, who won both league encounters last season. Despite two Gilzean headers, Dundee are 2-4 down with 27 minutes left. Two cracking shots by Wishart and Seith pull level, then 'The Gay Gordon' sparks a pitch invasion with his late strike.										
13	A	HIBERNIAN		1	W	3-1	1-0	Gilzean 45, Penman 49, Smith 80	Liney	Hamilton	Cox	Seith	Ure	Wishart	Smith	Penman	Cousin	Gilzean	Robertson
	25/11		*16,000*	*16*	24			*Stevenson 50*	*Simpson*	*Grant*	*McClelland*	*Preston*	*Easton*	*Baxter*	*Fraser*	*Stevenson*	*Baker*	*Kinloch*	*McLeod*
								Ref: W Syme (Glasgow)	Cox loses the toss and has to play down the Easter Road slope first. Smith, returning to the ground where he won the league as part of the Hibs Famous Five in 1952, scores direct from a corner and wins the man of the match. Dundee's win in Edinburgh is first in capital for three years.										
14	H	STIRLING ALB		1	D	2-2	1-2	Robertson 3, Cousin 52	Liney	Hamilton	Cox	Seith	Ure	Wishart	Smith	Penman	Cousin	Gilzean	Robertson
	2/12		**11,500**	*18*	25			*Lawlor 4, Sinclair 27*	*Brown*	*McGuinness*	*Pettigrew*	*Rowan*	*Weir*	*Johnstone*	*Kilgannon*	*Sinclair*	*Gilmour*	*Spence*	*Lawlor*
								Ref: J Allan (Inverness)	Dundee are unchanged for the fifth consecutive time and draw their first league game of the season. Gilzean has a goal chopped off for pushing Sinclair before Cousin heads home a Smith cross. Lawlor also has two goals disallowed for offside and kicking the ball out of Liney's hands.										
15	H	AIRDRIE		1	W	**5-1**	1-0	Wishart 3, Smith 56, Cousin 65, [Robertson 80, 85]	Liney	Hamilton	Cox	Seith	Ure	Wishart	Smith	Penman	Cousin	McGeachie	Robertson
	16/12		**11,500**	*17*	27			*Caven 74*	*Dempster*	*Shanks*	*Keenan*	*Hosie*	*Hannah*	*McNeil*	*Murray*	*Storrie*	*Caven*	*Reid*	*Newlands*
								Ref: J Barclay (Kirkcaldy)	Smith moves to centre-forward when Gilzean misses out after unknowingly breaking his jaw against Stirling. Airdrie hit the post twice before Smith's strike puts Dundee two up. Cousin scores after a one-two with Robertson in the box then returns the favour for both of Shug's goals.										
16	A	ST MIRREN		1	D	1-1	1-1	Wishart 22	Liney	Hamilton	Cox	Seith	Ure	Wishart	Smith	Penman	Cousin	McGeachie	Robertson
	23/12		*11,000*	*12*	28			*Fernie 26*	*Brown*	*Doonan*	*Wilson*	*McLean*	*Clunie*	*McTavish*	*Henderson*	*Campbell*	*McDonald*	*Fernie*	*Rodger*
								Ref: J Paterson (Linlithgow)	Former Dees forward, Bobby Flavell takes charge of Saints for the first time. British Rail run football specials to Paisley for 16 /- but only 100 Dundee fans travel west. Wishart scores from a free-kick which goes through Saints wall, while Fernie's goal is a deflected shot off of Ian Ure.										
17	H	FALKIRK		1	W	2-1	1-0	Gilzean 40, 58	Liney	Hamilton	Cox	Seith	Ure	Wishart	Smith	Penman	Cousin	Gilzean	Robertson
	6/1		15,000	*17*	30			*Innes 82*	*Boag*	*Lambie*	*McIntosh*	*Peacock*	*Thomson*	*Pierson*	*Reid*	*Blues*	*Oliver*	*Innes*	*Ormond*
								Ref: J Blair (Paisley)	Gilzean returns against Alex McRae's side after his hairline fracture and wears sandshoes to combat the frozen Dens pitch. His ingenuity is rewarded with two goals from the edge of the box. Dundee move five points clear of second placed Partick and eight points ahead of Rangers.										
18	A	HEARTS		1	W	2-0	2-0	Cousin 15, Gilzean 32	Liney	Hamilton	Cox	Seith	Ure	Wishart	Smith	Penman	Cousin	Gilzean	Robertson
	13/1		*25,000*	*9*	32				*Marshall*	*Kirk*	*Holt*	*Ferguson*	*Polland*	*Cumming*	*Paton*	*Elliot*	*Wallace*	*Gordon*	*Hamilton*
								Ref: J Barclay (Kirkcaldy)	Tommy Walker makes seven changes from Hearts' midweek defeat to Rangers. Gordon Smith was in a car crash before the game but insists on playing and sets up both goals. Marshall does exercises on the edge of the box to keep warm but misses a Smith cross for to Cousin head in.										
19	H	ABERDEEN		1	W	2-1	1-1	Cousin 22, Penman 55p	Liney	Hamilton	Cox	Seith	Ure	Wishart	Smith	Penman	Cousin	Gilzean	Robertson
	17/1		16,000	*12*	34			*Mulhall 30*	*Ogston*	*Bennet*	*Cadenhead*	*Burns*	*Kinnell*	*Fraser*	*Hosie*	*Callaghan*	*Little*	*Pearson*	*Mulhall*
								Ref: A Crossman (Edinburgh)	Dundee gain revenge for their only defeat in the league to date. As at Pittodrie, there is controversy over a penalty incident. A Robertson cross hits Bennet in the arm and the ref gives a penalty despite strong protests from Tommy Pearson's men. Penman converts his fourth Dundee pen.										
20	H	THIRD LANARK		1	W	2-1	1-1	Penman 17p, Robertson 66	Liney	Hamilton	Cox	Seith	Ure	Wishart	Smith	Penman	Cousin	Gilzean	Robertson
	20/1		17,500	*8*	36			*Goodfellow 19*	*Robertson*	*McCallum*	*Lewis*	*Reilly*	*McCormack*	*Cunningham*	*Goodfellow*	*Hilley*	*Harley*	*Gray*	*Fletcher*
								Ref: A McKenzie (Coatbridge)	Penman's second spot-kick in four days is converted after a Lewis handball. Thirds, one of only three sides to have beaten The Dees all season, immediately level when Goodfellow intercepts a pass from Hamilton. Robertson heads home when a Smith cross finds him at the back post.										
21	H	ST JOHNSTONE		1	W	2-1	1-1	Gilzean 22, Penman 68	Liney	Hamilton	Cox	Seith	Ure	Wishart	Smith	Penman	Cousin	Gilzean	Robertson
	24/1		16,000	*14*	38			*McVittie 30*	*Taylor*	*McFadyen*	*Lachlan*	*Little*	*J Ferguson*	*Donlevy*	*McIntyre*	*Townsend*	*A Ferguson*	*McVittie*	*Townsend*
								Ref: J Barclay (Kirkcaldy)	Dundee go 20 games undefeated in all games including league, friendly and Dewar Shield matches. Future Man Utd boss Alex Ferguson is in Bobby Brown's line up. Gilzean's 18-yard strike is equalled by a similar shot from Matt McVittie. Liney makes several vital saves late on.										
22	A	KILMARNOCK		1	D	1-1	0-0	Cousin 88	Liney	Hamilton	**Brown**	Seith	Ure	Wishart	Smith	Penman	Cousin	Gilzean	Robertson
	3/2		*14,000*	*6*	39			*Kerr 64*	*McLaughlin*	*Richmond*	*Watson*	*Davidson*	*Toner*	*Beattie*	*Brown*	*Yard*	*Kerr*	*Mason*	*McIlroy*
								Ref: E Cowan (Glasgow)	Dundee announce that their official fan club has increased tenfold since the start of the season to 300 members. Willie Waddle's side go ahead when Kerr beats two players on the edge of the box and shoots. Cousin's late strike from close range strike sees several kids run onto the pitch.										
23	H	MOTHERWELL		1	L	1-3	1-0	Robertson 30	Liney	Hamilton	Brown	Seith	Ure	Wishart	Smith	Penman	Cousin	Gilzean	Robertson
	10/2		19,000	*7*	39			*Quinn 50, Roberts 53, Young 80*	*Wylie*	*Delaney*	*McCallum*	*Aitken*	*Martis*	*McCann*	*Young*	*Quinn*	*Roberts*	*Hunter*	*McPhee*
								Ref: W Syme (Glasgow)	Dundee lose their first home league game of the season against future Dundee manager Bobby Ancell's side to signal the start of an alarming slump. A Ure long ball sets up Robertson and Dundee relax. Quinn and Roberts are both unmarked in the box to score, then Young nods home.										

No	Date		Att	Pos	Pt	F-A	H-T	Scorers, Times, and Referees	1	2	3	4	5	6	7	8	9	10	11
24	A	PARTICK TH		1	L	**0-3**	0-2		Liney	Hamilton	Brown	Seith	Ure	Wishart	Smith	Penman	Cousin	Gilzean	Robertson
	24/2		*15,000*	*7*	39			*Duffy 8, 17, Hainey 55*	*Niven*	*Muir*	*Brown*	*Closs*	*McKinnon*	*Cunningham*	*Smith*	*McBride*	*Hainey*	*Duffy*	*McParland*
								Ref: R Davidson (Airdrie)	Dundee hit rock bottom with a lacklustre display at Firhill as they fail to score in the league for the first time this season. The Dees only have two shots on goal all afternoon. Duffy is twice given space in the box to score and Hainey nets rebound off post. Rangers cut lead to one point										
25	A	CELTIC		2	L	1-2	0-0	Wishart 55	Liney	Hamilton	Cox	Seith	Ure	Brown	Smith	Wishart	Cousin	Gilzean	Robertson
	3/3		***39,000***	*3*	39			*Brogan 80, McNeil 85*	*Haffney*	*McKay*	*Kennedy*	*Crerand*	*McNeil*	*Price*	*Brogan*	*Lennox*	*Hughes*	*Divers*	*Carroll*
								Ref: R Rodger (Stonehouse)	Future Scotland manager Craig Brown moves to left-half upon skipper Cox's return. Bobby Lennox makes Celtic debut. The Dees lead when Wishart scores from 20 yards but Smith is hirpling from thigh injury. Brogan levels from 18 yards. Captain Billy McNeil heads a late winner.										
26	H	DUNFERMLINE		2	L	1-2	1-1	Seith 36	Liney	Hamilton	Cox	Seith	Ure	Brown	Penman	Wishart	Cousin	Gilzean	Robertson
	7/3		17,000	*4*	39			*Cunningham 23, Melrose 68*	*Connachan*	*Fraser*	*Cunningham*	*Mailer*	*Williamson*	*Miller*	*McDonald*	*Peebles*	*D Smith*	*A Smith*	*Melrose*
								Ref: W Brittle (Glasgow)	Without Smith, Dundee lack the guile to penetrate Dunfermline's well-organised sweeper system, masterminded by Northern Ireland full-back Cunningham, who heads home a corner. Seith combines with Wishart to score. Melrose's volley leaves Dundee three points behind Rangers.										
27	H	RANGERS		2	D	0 -0	0-0		Liney	Hamilton	Cox	Seith	Ure	Brown	Smith	Penman	Waddell	Cousin	Robertson
	14/3		**35,000**	*1*	40				*Ritchie*	*Shearer*	*Caldow*	*Davis*	*Paterson*	*Stevenson*	*Scott*	*McMillan*	*Christie*	*Brand*	*Wilson*
								Ref: J Barclay (Kirkcaldy)	Gilzean is out with flu but Smith leaves his North Berwick home at 6.30am to declare himself fit. Scot Symon fails in his application to have Jim Baxter released from an Army v Navy match in Aldershot. Dundee end a run of four defeats to keep their slim championship hopes alive.										
28	A	RAITH		2	W	3-2	1-1	Cousin 13, Penman 63, 82	Liney	Hamilton	Cox	Seith	Ure	Brown	Smith	Penman	Waddell	Cousin	Robertson
	17/3		*5,000*	*16*	42			*Gilfillian 4, 56*	*Thorburn*	*Stevenson*	*Mochan*	*Stein*	*Forysth*	*McGuire*	*Adamson*	*Kerr*	*Gilfillan*	*McFadzean*	*Urquhart*
								Ref: J Stewart (Paisley)	Dundee get back to winning ways but survive two first-half Raith penalty claims when the ball strikes Ure's arm on both occassions. Dundee subject Hugh Shaw's men to an arial bombardment and it pays dividends when Penman heads home two crosses from Robertson and Smith.										
29	H	HIBERNIAN		2	W	1-0	0-0	Waddell 52	Liney	Hamilton	Cox	Seith	Ure	Brown	Smith	Penman	Waddell	Cousin	Wishart
	24/3		12,000	*11*	44				*Simpson*	*Grant*	*McClelland*	*Preston*	*Easton*	*McLeod*	*Scott*	*Baker*	*Fraser*	*Stevenson*	*Kinloch*
								Ref: W Elliot (Barrhead)	Waddell consigns Walter Galbraith's side to defeat with his first goal of the season on a wet and windy afternoon. He chases a long ball from Seith to shoot past Simpson from 10 yards. Dundee receive a massive boost when Jerry Kerr's United shock Rangers with a 1-0 win at Ibrox.										
30	A	STIRLING ALB		1	W	3-2	2-2	Cousin 21, Smith 40, Gilzean 68	Liney	Hamilton	Cox	Seith	Ure	Brown	Smith	Gilzean	Waddell	Cousin	Robertson
	31/3		***4,500***	18	46			*McDonald 26, Munn 41*	*Brown*	*Currie*	*McGuiness*	*McGregor*	*Weir*	*Johnstone*	*McDonald*	*Gilmour*	*Munn*	*Wilson*	*Spence*
								Ref: W Mullan (Cardenden)	Shankly celebrates his daughter's engagement to Utd left back Johnny Briggs by capturing top spot with Rangers playing in Scottish Cup semi. A poor Anfield crowd sees Gilzean mark his return with the winning header from a Robertson corner against Sammy Forsyth's basement boys.										
31	A	AIRDRIE		2	W	2-1	1-1	Penman 32, 50p	Liney	Hamilton	Cox	Seith	Ure	Wishart	Smith	Penman	Cousin	Gilzean	Robertson
	7/4		*7,000*	*16*	48			*Murray 45*	*Dempster*	*Jonquin*	*Shanks*	*Reid*	*Hannah*	*Thomson*	*Murray*	*Storrie*	*Tees*	*Newlands*	*Duncan*
								Ref: W Brittle (Glasgow)	Rangers' midweek win at Perth put them back to the top. Trainer Sammy Kean misses the match through illness. Penalty king Penman keeps his 100% spot record after Shanks fists the ball over the bar. Dundee players surround the ref, who consults his linesman and awards the kick.										
32	A	DUNDEE UTD		2	W	2-1	1-1	Gilzean 44, 86	Liney	Hamilton	Cox	Seith	Ure	Wishart	Smith	Penman	Cousin	Gilzean	Robertson
	9/4		*20,000*	*9*	50			*Irvine 15*	*Ugolini*	*Gordon*	*Briggs*	*Neilson*	*Smith*	*Fraser*	*Carlyle*	*Millar*	*Gillespie*	*Irvine*	*Mochan*
								Ref: W Mullan (Cardenden)	Easter Monday Derby Day is significant in the championship race as Dundee pull level with Rangers who draw 1-1 with Celtic. A capacity Tannadice crowd sees Jim Irvine put Utd ahead with a header. Gilzean scores winner with a 25-yard thunderbolt which bounces over Ugolini.										
33	H	ST MIRREN		1	W	2-0	1-0	Cousin 42, Penman 82	Liney	Hamilton	Cox	Seith	Ure	Wishart	Smith	Penman	Cousin	Gilzean	Robertson
	25/4		20,000	*15*	52				*Brown*	*Doonan*	*Wilson*	*Stewart*	*Clunie*	*McTavish*	*Henderson*	*McLean*	*Beck*	*Fernie*	*Millar*
								Ref: W Syme (Glasgow)	Liney is the hero when he saves a penalty from Clunie in 78 minutes after Smith handled. Penman seals victory shortly afterwards and fans invade the pitch when the tannoy announces Rangers lost 0-1 at Pittodrie leaving Dundee needing a point against St Johnstone in the last game.										
34	A	ST JOHNSTONE		1	W	3-0	1-0	Gilzean 24, 59, Penman 67	Liney	Hamilton	Cox	Seith	Ure	Wishart	Smith	Penman	Cousin	Gilzean	Robertson
	28/4		26,500	*17*	54				*Taylor*	*McFadyen*	*Lachlan*	*Little*	*J Ferguson*	*Donlevy*	*McIntyre*	*Townsend*	*McVittie*	*A Ferguson*	*Thomson*
	Average	Home 17,206	Away 16,147					Ref: E Cowan (Glasgow)	Saints just need a point to stay up on a gloriously hot day. Gilzean heads home from a Smith cross and then finishes a brilliant long ball from Hamilton. Penman crashes third in off the bar and chaos reigns at final whistle when thousands invade the pitch to salute the league champions.										

League Cup – Section 2				F-A	H-T	Scorers, Times, and Referees	1	2	3	4	5	6	7	8	9	10	11
2	H	AIRDRIE 12/8	W	2-0	1-0	Wishart 3, Cousin 51	Liney	Hamilton	Cox	Seith	Ure	Wishart	McGeachie	Penman	Cousin	Gilzean	Robertson
		13,000	2				*Beaton*	*Shanks*	*Kennan*	*Stewart*	*Johnstone*	*NcNeill*	*Newlands*	*Storrie*	*Caven*	*Rankine*	*Duncan*
						Ref: W Mullan (Cardenden)	The crowd got their three shillings admission's worth with Dundee's fast incisive football, and a Wishart strike from edge of the box gave The Dees their first goal of the season. Cousin was getting stick from the crowd for his missed chances but silenced them with a close-range finish.										
2	A	RANGERS 16/8	L	2-4	2-2	Penman 28, Cousin 37	Liney	Hamilton	Cox	Seith	Ure	Wishart	McGeachie	Penman	Waddell	Cousin	Robertson
		40,000	2			*Brand 12, 13, Wilson 71, Millar 84*	*Ritchie*	*Shearer*	*Caldow*	*Davis*	*Paterson*	*Baxter*	*Scott*	*McMillan*	*Millar*	*Brand*	*Wilson*
						Ref: G Mitchell (Falkirk)	Dundee come from two goals down when Penman and Cousin equalise a Ralph Brand double. Dundee attack but miss finishing of Gilzean who failed a late fitness test. Wilson restores Gers' lead after a mazy dribble past three players and go top of the section after a Millar late header.										
2	A	THIRD LANARK 19/8	L	2-3	1-1	Smith 31, Gilzean 55	Liney	Hamilton	Cox	Seith	Ure	Wishart	Smith	Penman	Gilzean	Cousin	Robertson
		12,000	2			*Harley 5, 57, Wishart 50 (og)*	*Robertson*	*McGillvray*	*Lewis*	*Reilly*	*McCormack*	*Robb*	*Goodfellow*	*Hilley*	*Harley*	*Gray*	*McInnes*
						Ref J Holburn (Edinburgh)	Gordon Smith notches his first goal for Dundee when he equalises after a one-two with Cousin. Gilzean, who got 13 League cup goals last year opens his account for the season with a close-range header. Wishart deflects a Gray shot past Liney to put Thirds above Dundee in the section.										
2	A	AIRDRIE 26/8	W	5-0	1-0	Cousin 27, Smith 67, Penman 81, [Gilzean 85, 90]	Liney	Hamilton	Cox	Seith	Ure	Wishart	Smith	Penman	Gilzean	Cousin	Robertson
		4,500	4				*Beaton*	*Shanks*	*Keenan*	*Hinkelswood*	*Johnstone*	*McNeill*	*Newlands*	*Hawkshaw*	*Tees*	*Rankin*	*Duncan*
						Ref: W. Brittle (Glasgow)	Dundee's five-goal victory is revenge for Hamilton, Cox, Cousin and Robertson, who played in a 1-7 defeat at Broomfield four years ago. Two crosses for late Gilzean headers and a goal from a set piece is beginning to show the 37 year old Gordon Smith's importance to the Dark Blues.										
2	H	RANGERS 30/8	D	1-1	1-1	Robertson 3	Liney	Hamilton	Cox	Seith	Ure	Wishart	Smith	Penman	Gilzean	Cousin	Robertson
		24,000	5			*Brand 31*	*Ritchie*	*Shearer*	*Caldow*	*Davis*	*Paterson*	*Baxter*	*Scott*	*McMillan*	*Christie*	*Brand Wilson*	
						Ref; A Cook (Edinburgh)	Rangers have already qualified but go behind when right-half Davis loses the ball to Cousin, who squares to Robertson, who scores. The Dees claim for a penalty seconds after Brand equalised and Gilzean has a goal chopped off late on when the ref had already blown for a free-kick.										
2	H	THIRD LANARK 2/9	D	2-2	1-1	Cousin 40, Penman 64	Liney	Hamilton	Cox	Seith	Ure	Wishart	Smith	Penman	Gilzean	Cousin	Robertson
		9,000	6			*Gray 41, 89*	*Robertson*	*McGillvray*	*Lewis*	*Robb*	*McCormack*	*Cunningham*	*Bryce*	*Hilley*	*Goodfellow*	*Gray*	*McInnes*
						Ref: J Mackie (East Kilbride)	A late Thirds goal revives memories of 1949, when a last-minute equaliser cost Dundee a point when they lost the league on the last day. After fans invaded the pitch on Wednesday, the tannoy announcer made an unnecessary appeal at half-time for fans to stay on the terracing today.										

Qual	Rangers	6	5	1	0	18	5	11
	DUNDEE	6	2	2	2	14	10	6
	Third Lanark	6	2	2	2	10	14	6
	Airdrie	6	0	1	5	5	18	1

Scottish Cup						F-A	H-T	Scorers, Times, and Referees	1	2	3	4	5	6	7	8	9	10	11
2	H	ST MIRREN		1	L	0-1	0-1		Liney	Hamilton	Cox	Seith	Ure	Wishart	Smith	Penman	Cousin	Gilzean	Robertson
	27/1		22,834	*12*				*McLean 38*	*Brown*	*Doonan*	*Wilson*	*Stewart*	*Clunie*	*McTavish*	*Henderson*	*McLean*	*Beck*	*Fernie*	*Millar*
								Ref: R Davidson (Airdrie)	After receiving a bye in the first round, Dundee face the Buddies in the Cup for the first time since they won 2-1 in 1949. Bobby Flavell gives his team talk during a morning walk on Brought Ferry beach, and a George McLean six-yard shot against the run of play takes them through.										

	P	W	D	L	F	A	W	D	L	F	A	Pts
		Home					Away					
1 DUNDEE	34	13	2	2	41	23	12	2	3	39	23	54
2 Rangers	34	12	2	3	43	18	10	5	2	41	13	51
3 Celtic	34	12	4	1	45	16	7	4	6	35	21	46
4 Dunfermline	34	13	1	3	45	15	6	4	7	31	31	43
5 Kilmarnock	34	10	4	3	41	27	6	6	5	33	31	42
6 Hearts	34	7	5	5	30	28	9	1	7	24	21	38
7 Partick Th	34	12	0	5	38	21	4	3	10	24	34	35
8 Hibernian	34	7	5	5	31	30	7	0	10	27	42	33
9 Motherwell	34	7	3	7	35	34	6	3	8	30	28	32
10 Dundee Utd	34	8	3	6	43	30	5	3	9	27	41	32
11 Third Lanark	34	8	3	6	37	31	5	2	10	22	29	31
12 Aberdeen	34	6	6	5	33	27	4	3	10	27	46	29
13 Raith Rovers	34	5	5	7	24	24	5	2	10	27	44	27
14 Falkirk	34	6	2	9	23	30	5	2	10	22	38	26
15 Airdrie	34	7	2	8	35	33	2	5	10	22	45	25
16 St Mirren	34	7	3	7	29	29	3	2	12	23	51	25
17 St Johnstone	34	4	2	11	14	34	5	5	7	21	27	25
18 Stirling Alb	34	5	3	9	22	37	1	3	13	12	44	18
	612	149	55	102	609	487	102	55	149	487	609	612

Odds & ends

Double wins: (7) Falkirk, Dundee Utd, Hearts, Third Lanark, Raith, Hibs, Airdrie.
Double losses: (0)

Won from behind: (6) Kilmarnock (h), Dunfermline (a), Partick (h), Raith (h), Raith (a), Dundee Utd (a).
Lost from in front: (2) Motherwell (h), Celtic (a).

High Spots: Winning 4-1 v Dundee Utd in first home league match.
Going 20 league games undefeated from August to mid-February.
Winning 5-1 v title rivals Rangers at Ibrox in November.
Clinching League Championship in Perth on last day of the season.

Low spots: Losing at home 0-1 v St Mirren in Scottish Cup 2nd round.
Losing four league games in a row in February and March.

Hat-tricks: (2) Gilzean, Penman.
Ever presents: (5) Cousin, Hamilton, Liney, Seith, Ure.
Leading scorer: Gilzean (24).

	Appearances Lge	LC	SC	Goals Lge	LC	SC	Tot
Brown, Craig	**9**						
Cousin, Alan	**34**	6	1	**15**	4		**19**
Cox, Bobby	**31**	6	1				
Gilzean, Alan	**29**	5	1	**24**	3		**27**
Hamilton, Alan	**34**	6	1				
Liney, Pat	**34**	6	1				
McGeachie, George	**3**	2					
Penman, Andy	**32**	6	1	**17**	3		**20**
Robertson, Hugh	**33**	6	1	**6**	1		**7**
Seith, Bobby	**34**	6	1	**2**			**2**
Smith, Gordon	**32**	4	1	**7**	2		**9**
Stuart, Alex	**2**						
Ure, Ian	**34**	6	1				
Waddell, Bobby	**4**	1		**1**			**1**
Wishart, Bobby	**29**	6	1	**6**	1		**7**
(own-goals)				**2**			**2**
15 players used	**374**	**66**	**11**	**80**	**14**		**94**

SCOTTISH DIVISION 1 — Manager: Bob Shankly — SEASON 1962-63

No	Date	Opponent	Att	Pos	Pt	F-A	H-T	Scorers, Times, and Referees	1	2	3	4	5	6	7	8	9	10	11
1	A	HEARTS			L	1-3	0-1	Houston 60	**Slater**	Hamilton	Cox	Seith	Ure	Wishart	Smith	Penman	Waddell	Cousin	**Houston**
	22/8		*18,000*		0			*Davidson 36, 61, 72*	*Marshall*	*Polland*	*Holt*	*Ferguson*	*Barry*	*Cumming*	*Rodger*	*Paton*	*Davidson*	*Wallace*	*Hamilton*
								Ref: T Wharton (Glasgow)	Hearts win their third game in a row against the two Dundee sides. Davidson converts after Hamilton clears a shot off the line. Houston nets a Waddell cut-back but from the restart Davidson scores from 20 yards out. A Paton through ball splits the Dundee defence to set up the hat-trick.										
2	H	ABERDEEN		13	D	2-2	1-2	Penman 40, Gilzean 90	Slater	Hamilton	Cox	Seith	Ure	Wishart	Smith	Penman	Cousin	Gilzean	Robertson
	8/9		**18,000**	*6*	1			*Cooke 11, Winchester 42*	*Ogston*	*Bennett*	*Hogg*	*Kinnell*	*Coutts*	*Smith*	*Cummings*	*Allan*	*Winchester*	*Cooke*	*Mulhall*
								Ref: J Barclay (Kirkcaldy)	Ogston saves penalty from Penman after Dons left-back Dave Smith, younger brother of United's Doug Smith, had handled. Future Dark Blue hero Charlie Cooke scores when he beats Cox and fires past Slater. Kinnell man-marks Gilzean, but he nets a late header from a Penman cross.										
3	A	DUNDEE UTD		12	D	1-1	1-1	Cousin 15	Slater	Hamilton	Cox	Seith	Ure	Wishart	Smith	Penman	Cousin	Gilzean	Robertson
	15/9		*18,000*	*16*	2			*Carlyle 11p*	*Davie*	*Miller*	*Gordon*	*Neilson*	*Smith*	*Fraser*	*Carlyle*	*Howieson*	*Gillespie*	*Irvine*	*Riddle*
								Ref: A Webster (Throsk)	Carlyle scores from the spot after Seith impedes Irvine in the box. Skipper Cox is booked for a foul on Caryle, spotted by the linesman. Cousin scores his first goal in 16 matches when Penman tees him up 18 yards out. Gilzean hits the crossbar three times and Gordon clears off the line.										
4	H	CLYDE		10	W	2-0	0-0	Penman 50, 64	Slater	Hamilton	Cox	Seith	Ure	Stuart	Smith	Penman	Cousin	Gilzean	Robertson
	22/9		12,000	*15*	4				*McCulloch*	*Gray*	*Finnigan*	*White*	*Finlay*	*McHugh*	*Grant*	*Thomson*	*McLaughlin*	*Steel*	*Colrain*
								Ref: J Paterson (Bothwell)	Gilzean is frustrated after several angled shots are saved by McCulloch. He goes to the bench and asks Shankly for an extra £5 if he manages to score. Penman secures Dundee's first league win with two edge-of-the-box strikes but is ticked off by the referee after he clashes with White.										
5	A	RANGERS		9	D	1-1	0-0	Shearer 73 (og)	Liney	Hamilton	Cox	Seith	Ure	Wishart	Smith	Penman	Cousin	Gilzean	Robertson
	29/9		***46,000***	*3*	5			*Millar 55*	*Ritchie*	*Shearer*	*Caldow*	*Davis*	*McKinnon*	*Baxter*	*Henderson*	*Greig*	*Millar*	*Brand*	*Wilson*
								Ref: R Davidson (Airdrie)	Scottish selectors are present to watch Ian Ure and see Dundee extend their six-year unbeaten league run at Ibrox. Henderson double shuffles on the wing to cross for Millar to head home. Cousin's cross is mis-hit by Shearer to Robertson who shoots into the net off the Rangers captain.										
6	H	FALKIRK		8	W	2-1	1-1	Cousin 20, Gilzean 77	Slater	Hamilton	Cox	Seith	Ure	Wishart	Smith	Penman	Cousin	Gilzean	Robertson
	6/10		12,000	*14*	7			*Adam 38*	*Whigham*	*Rae*	*Hunter*	*Pierson*	*Lowry*	*McIntosh*	*Blues*	*Redpath*	*Henderson*	*Reid*	*Adam*
								Ref; F Crossley (Wishaw)	The ref's coin is stolen by two charity collectors who run on the pitch and pick it up after he tosses it. Cousin is left wide open in the box to score. Adam scores when he collects ball after Hamilton and Seith collide. Whigham fails to cut out a Penman cross and Gilzean heads home.										
7	A	HIBERNIAN		8	D	2-2	0-1	Penman 61, Cousin 76	Slater	Hamilton	Cox	Seith	Ure	Wishart	Smith	Penman	Cousin	Gilzean	Robertson
	13/10		*5,000*	*16*	8			*Byrne 30, Baker 82*	*Simpson*	*Fraser*	*McLelland*	*Grant*	*Easton*	*McLeod*	*Scott*	*Byrne*	*Baker*	*M Stevenson*	*E Stevenson*
								Ref: J Hamilton (Renfrew)	Dundee claim Byrne is offside when he scored from 12 yards but their protests are ignored. Penman and Cousin both score with shots from the edge of the box. Dundee contest Hibs' second as players jostle in the centre-circle, claiming Baker fouled Slater when jumping for a high ball.										
8	H	KILMARNOCK		7	W	1-0	1-0	Gilzean 9	Slater	Reid	Cox	Seith	**Ryden**	Wishart	Smith	Penman	Cousin	Gilzean	Robertson
	20/10		16,000	*9*	10				*McLaughlin*	*King*	*Watson*	*O'Connor*	*McGrory*	*Beattie*	*Black*	*McInally*	*Kerr*	*Sneddon*	*McIlroy*
								Ref: A McKenzie (Coatbridge)	Lisbon manager Armando Ferreria is among the crowd and 17,000 tickets are sold for the home leg after the match. Dundee score with a six-man move which starts with Cox in his own box and is finished by Gilzean close in. Penman hits the post after Gilzean puts him clean through.										
9	A	DUNFERMLINE		7	L	0-2	0-1		Slater	Hamilton	Cox	Seith	Ure	Wishart	Smith	Penman	Cousin	Gilzean	Houston
	27/10		*9,000*	*4*	10			*Sinclair 10, Smith 55*	*Herriot*	*Callaghan*	*Cunningham*	*Thomson*	*MacLean*	*Miller*	*McLindon*	*Smith*	*Paton*	*Sinclair*	*Melrose*
								Ref: G McColville (Wishaw)	Sinclair slips past Ure in the box to score. Gilzean hits the post in 48 minutes with a free-kick and then heads a Houston cross onto the post five minutes later. Wishart's body deflects Smith's shot past Slater. Herriot pulls a muscle and goes off with 20 minutes left and Miller goes in goal.										
10	H	AIRDRIE		8	W	2-1	2-1	Houston 15, Gilzean 19	Slater	Hamilton	Cox	Seith	Ure	Wishart	Smith	Penman	Cousin	Gilzean	Houston
	3/11		12,000	*15*	12			*Duncan 44*	*Samson*	*Shanks*	*Keenan*	*Stewart*	*Hannah*	*Reid*	*Newlands*	*Rowan*	*Tees*	*Duncan*	*Coats*
								Ref: J Stewart (Paisley)	Houston scores with an angular drive from the left and Gilzean heads home a Smith cross. Hannah heads over his own bar but the ref gives a goal-kick to the Diamonds from which Tees flicks to Duncan who volleys home. Dundee fans jeer and criticise Slater's kicking throughout.										
11	A	PARTICK TH		8	L	0-1	0-0		Slater	Hamilton	Cox	Seith	Ure	Wishart	Smith	Penman	Cousin	Gilzean	Houston
	10/11		*18,000*	*2*	12			*Brown 75p*	*Niven*	*Hogan*	*Brown*	*McParland*	*Harvey*	*Cunningham*	*Cowan*	*Whitlaw*	*Hainey*	*Duffy*	*Smith*
								Ref: W Fyfe (Edinburgh)	Shankly's predecessor Willie Thornton is in charge of the Firhill side. Dundee protest a dubious handball decision against Seith in the box but Brown scores the resultant kick. Niven saves at the feet of both Gilzean and Penman late on and Houston hits the bar after nutmegging Hogan.										

12	H	CELTIC	8	D	0-0	0-0		Slater	Hamilton	Cox	Seith	Ure	Wishart	Smith	Penman	Gilzean	Cousin	Houston
17/11		**18,000**	*4*	13				*Haffey*	*Young*	*Kennedy*	*Crerand*	*McNeil*	*O'Neil*	*Murdoch*	*Craig*	*Divers*	*Gallacher*	*Byrne*
							Ref: J Rodger (Stonehouse)	Dens Park passes a late pitch inspection despite being snow-covered and frost-bitten. Dundee fans in the Provie Road terracing throw snowballs at Haffey at the start of the second half. A 30-yard Wishart thunderbolt cannons off the post. McNeil heads a Houston cross against his own bar.										
13	A	THIRD LANARK	10	L	3-4	1-4	Cousin 3, Gilzean 84, 90	Slater	Hamilton	Cox	Seith	Ure	Wishart	Smith	Penman	Gilzean	Cousin	Houston
24/11		*5,000*	*13*	13			*Reilly 4, Gray 23, 30, Spence 44*	*Robertson*	*McGillvray*	*Cunningham*	*Reilly*	*McCormack*	*Baird*	*Bryce*	*Spence*	*Grant*	*Gray*	*McInnes*
							Ref: J Kelly (Motherwell)	Dundee players argue and shout with each other at the start of the second half after George Young's side capitalise on poor Dundee's first-half defending. A well-timed Baird tackle stops Penman equalising. Dundee score their highest number of goals in the league or cup and still lose.										
14	H	QUEEN OF SOUTH	8	W	**10-2**	7-2	Gilzean 1,12,20,28,41,45,55, Penman 33,	Slater	Hamilton	Cox	Ryden	Ure	Wishart	Smith	Penman	Cousin	Gilzean	Houston
1/12		12,000	*9*	15			*Murphy 3, 40* [Ryden 72, Houston 73]	*Farm*	*Morrison*	*Kerr*	*Irving*	*Rugg*	*Murphy*	*Hannigan*	*Martin*	*Frye*	*Anderson*	*Murray*
							Ref: A Crossman (Edinburgh)	Fog makes visibility very poor for players and fans. Queen's keeper Farm collides with Gilzean, is out cold for five minutes and is stretchered off in the twelfth minute and rushed to hospital. Gilzean is one short of Celtic's Jimmy McGrory's league record of eight goals in one game.										
15	A	ST MIRREN	8	W	3-0	1-0	Campbell R 3 (og), Cousin80, Penman 87	Slater	Hamilton	Cox	Ryden	Ure	Wishart	McGeachie	Penman	Cousin	Gilzean	Houston
8/12		*11,000*	*11*	17				*Williamson*	*Murray*	*Wilson*	*Campbell R*	*Clunie*	*McTavish*	*Campbell B*	*McLean*	*White*	*Queen*	*Robertson*
							Ref: G Bowman (Clydebank)	Heavy rain makes visibility so bad that Slater claims he heard rather than saw a Saints freekick hit the bar. 'Red' Campbell overhits a pass back to his own keeper and it flies into the net. Black Campbell hits Slater's post between Cousin's close-range effort and Penman's 20-yard strike.										
16	H	MOTHERWELL	8	D	2-2	0-0	Gilzean 75, Wishart 86	Slater	Hamilton	Cox	Ryden	Ure	Wishart	Smith	Penman	Cousin	Gilzean	Houston
15/12		13,000	*14*	18			*Roberts 72, 80*	*Wyllie*	*Thomson*	*McCallum*	*Aitken*	*Martis*	*Roberts*	*Lindsay*	*McBride*	*Russell*	*McCann*	*Weir*
							Ref; W Syme (Glasgow)	Well boss Bobby Ancell is destined to be Shankly's successor when he leaves in two years A gale-force wind helps Roberts hit two free kicks through the Dundee wall and into the net. Wishart scores first league goal of the season with a tap in. Gilzean hits the bar after Dundee equalise.										
17	A	RAITH ROVERS	7	W	4-2	0-2	Gilzean 69, 85, 87, Penman 90p	Slater	Hamilton	Cox	Ryden	Ure	Wishart	Smith	Penman	Gilzean	Houston	Robertson
22/12		*5,000*	*18*	20			*Smith 14, Caven 26*	*Thorburn*	*Stevenson*	*Haig*	*Stein*	*Forysth*	*Clinton*	*McDonald*	*Smith*	*Caven*	*Aitken*	*Adamson*
							Ref: J Gearie (East Kilbride)	McDonald tackles Smith twice and sets up two goals. Shankly shuffles the attack. Thorburn drops the ball Gilzean's feet so he can give The Dees the lead. Aitken handles and Penman penalty seals win. Dundee travel on the train and Gilzean tells fans that they can still catch Rangers.										
18	A	ABERDEEEN	8	L	0-1	0-1		Slater	Hamilton	Cox	Ryden	Ure	Wishart	Smith	Penman	Cousin	Gilzean	Houston
1/1		*22,000*	*6*	20			*Winchester 36*	*Ogston*	*Bennett*	*Hogg*	*Kinnell*	*Coutts*	*Smith*	*Cummings*	*Allan*	*Winchester*	*Cooke*	*Thom*
							Ref: J Barclay (Kirkcaldy)	The ref speaks to the police when he is hit with snowballs by the Pittodrie crowd. Cooke is booked for retaliation after a Ryden tackle. Gilzean is then booked for a robust tackle on Cummings. Winchester nets with a knee-high drive after Cooke jinxes past Cox and Ure to set him up.										
19	A	CLYDE	8	L	2-3	1-0	Gilzean 15, 60	Slater	Hamilton	Cox	Seith	Ure	Wishart	Smith	Penman	Cousin	Gilzean	Houston
5/1		*7,000*	*15*	20			*Colrain 59, McFarlane 70, Hughes 82*	*McCulloch*	*Gray*	*Blain*	*Murray*	*Malloy*	*Currie*	*McLean*	*Reid*	*McFarlane*	*Colrain*	*Hughes*
							Ref: J Stewart (Paisley)	Ure survives a late fitness test but a moment of indecision allows Colrain to nip in and score. Gilzean restores Dundee's lead after a one-two with Cousin but then slips on the muddy Shawfield pitch to let McFarlane pull the Bully Wee level. Hughes out-jumps Hamilton for the third.										
20	A	AIRDRIE	10	L	0-1	0-0		Slater	Hamilton	Cox	Seith	Ure	Wishart	Smith	Penman	Waddell	Cousin	Robertson
9/3		*3,000*	*15*	20			*Duncan 72*	*Samson*	*Jonquin*	*Keenan*	*Hosie*	*Thomson*	*Reid*	*Tees*	*Rowan*	*McCall*	*Murray*	*Duncan*
							Ref: A Cook (Edinburgh)	Gilzean misses out at Broomfield after needing six stitches in a foot wound in Brussels. The Diamonds pressurise a tired-looking Dundee side and are rewarded when Duncan out-jumps Cox at the near post from Reid's cross. Dundee are now two and a half months without a league win.										
21	H	PARTICK TH	8	W	2-1	0-0	Hogan 55 (og), Cameron 77	Slater	Hamilton	Cox	Seith	Ure	Wishart	Penman	Waddell	**Cameron**	Cousin	Robertson
16/3		12,000	*2*	22			*Duffy 75*	*Niven*	*Hogan*	*Brown*	*McParland*	*McKinnon*	*Cunningham*	*Cowan*	*Whitelaw*	*Smith*	*Duffy*	*Gowlay*
							Ref: T Hamilton (Renfrew)	A strong cross-wind spoils the game. Waddell's cross strikes right-back Hogan on the chest and flies into his own net. Niven saves with his feet when Cousin is in on goal. Current Dees youth coach Kenny Cameron scores his first Dark Blue goal with an angular shot into the far corner.										
22	A	CELTIC	9	L	**1-4**	0-3	Gilzean 61 *[Craig 81]*	Slater	Hamilton	Cox	Seith	Ure	Wishart	Smith	Penman	Cousin	Gilzean	Robertson
23/3		*42,000*	*4*	22			*Hughes 21, Brogan 33, Seith 38 (og),*	*Haffey*	*McKay*	*Kennedy*	*McNamee*	*McNeil*	*Price*	*Murdoch*	*Craig*	*Hughes*	*Divers*	*Brogan*
							Ref: W Fyfe (Edinburgh)	Celtic Chairmen Bob Kelly tells the press that Dundee would have won if they had taken their chances. Ian Ure complains that he is fouled by Hughes when he heads in a corner kick. Slater and Hamilton collide from a Craig corner and Brogan glances the ball home with his head.										
23	A	QUEEN OF SOUTH	10	L	0-1	0-1		Slater	Reid	Cox	Seith	Ryden	Wishart	Smith	Penman	Cousin	Gilzean	Robertson
5/4		*5,500*	*12*	22			*McLean 13*	*Farm*	*Morrison*	*McTurk*	*Kerr*	*Rugg*	*Anderson*	*Hannigan*	*Frye*	*Paterson*	*Samson*	*McLean*
							Ref: D Weir (Glasgow)	The Doonhamers win against Dundee for the first time in five years. Queens play with strong wind in their favour in the first half. Slater misses a Hannigan corner and McLean hits into the empty net. Frye's lob is headed onto bar by Paterson. Gilzean's goal is ruled offside in 84 minutes.										

No	Date		Att	Pos	Pt	F-A	H-T	Scorers, Times, and Referees	1	2	3	4	5	6	7	8	9	10	11
24	H	HIBERNIAN		10	L	1-3	0-2	Penman 67p	Slater	Hamilton	Cox	Seith	Ure	Wishart	Smith	Penman	Gilzean	Cousin	Robertson
	8/4		10,000	*15*	22			*Ure 33 (og), Baker 39, 58*	*Simpson*	*Cameron*	*McCleeland*	*Grant*	*Toner*	*Leishman*	*O'Rourke*	*Falconer*	*Baker*	*Preston*	*Stevenson*
								Ref: W Elliot (Barrhead)	Dundee lose their first home league game of the season. Stevenson's shot hits Ure and sends Slater the wrong way. Baker nets a loose ball off the post. Robertson is fouled by Cameron in the box and Penman hits the penalty in off the post. The referee orders a retake and Penman scores										
25	H	ST MIRREN		10	W	5-1	3-1	Houston 6, Waddell 40, 47, 66, Gilzean 43	Slater	Reid	Cox	Seith	Ure	Wishart	Smith	Penman	Waddell	Gilzean	Houston
	13/4		10,000	*13*	24			*Beck 29*	*Beattie*	*Murray*	*Riddell*	*Campbell*	*Clunie*	*McTavish*	*Ross*	*Kerrigan*	*White*	*Beck*	*McGhee*
								Ref: G Bowman (Clydebank)	Milan spy, Swede Nils Liedholm, is in the crowd. Six inches of snow is cleared off the pitch beforehand. Dundee play with a strong wind and Clunie gifts Waddell the ball in the box to score. Gilzean nets a scorcher from 25 yards. Dundee's defence gets in a fankle and Beck capitalises.										
26	H	DUNDEE UTD		11	L	1-2	1-1	Waddell 19	Slater	Hamilton	Cox	Seith	Ure	Wishart	Smith	Penman	Waddell	Gilzean	Houston
	15/4		16,000	*7*	24			*Mochan 43, Mitchell 55*	*Davie*	*Gordon*	*Roe*	*Fraser*	*Smith*	*Briggs*	*Brodie*	*Gillespie*	*Mochan*	*Millar*	*Mitchell*
								Ref: T Wharton (Glasgow)	Kick-off is delayed 10 minutes to allow the ref to inspect the waterlogged pitch. Ure is booked for a foul on Mochan who hits a free-kick in off the wall. 16-year-old Mitchell wins a Brodie cross on the bye-line and walks the ball into the net to give Utd their first ever league win at Dens.										
27	A	MOTHERWELL		11	L	1-2	0-1	Gilzean 47	Slater	Hamilton	Cox	Seith	Ure	Wishart	Smith	Penman	Cousin	Gilzean	Houston
	20/4		*8,500*	*9*	24			*McCann 37, Lindsay 89*	*Wyllie*	*Thomson*	*McCallum*	*Aitken*	*Martis*	*Roberts*	*Lindsay*	*McCann*	*McBride*	*Goodwin*	*Weir*
								Ref: J Stewart (Paisley)	Cox fouls Lindsay on the edge of the box. Roberts floats the kick to McCann who catches Slater flat-footed. Ure claims he is fouled but dithers on a long ball and Lindsay nips in to score. Gilzean nods in a Smith cross. Cox damages a cartilage and will miss Monday's flight to Milan.										
28	H	RAITH ROVERS		13	D	1-1	1-0	Gilzean 40	Liney	Reid	Stuart	Seith	Ure	Wishart	Penman	Waddell	Cousin	Gilzean	Robertson
	27/4		9,000	*18*	25			*Lourie 62*	*Thorburn*	*Stevenson*	*Haig*	*Wilson*	*Bolton*	*Burrows*	*Lourie*	*McDonald*	*Gilfillan*	*Menzies*	*McGrogan*
								Ref: W Sime (Glasgow)	Raith are already relegated and hit the bar twice in the early stages. A long ball by Ure is nodded on by Cousin and smashed in by Gilzean. The Dees have the wind and slope advantage in the second half but Lourie is left completely unmarked in the box and strokes the ball past Liney.										
29	H	HEARTS		12	D	2-2	1-1	Penman 45p, 66	Slater	Hamilton	Stuart	Seith	Ure	Ryden	Smith	Penman	Waddell	Gilzean	Houston
	6/5		10,000	*12*	26			*Rodger 21, Wallace 87*	*Marshall*	*Shevlane*	*Holt*	*Ferguson*	*Barry*	*Higgins*	*Rodger*	*Hamilton*	*Paton*	*Wallace*	*Hamilton J*
								Ref: W Syme (Glasgow)	Rodger scores with a header from a Johnny Hamilton cross. Penman scores his fourth penalty of the season after Barry brings down Houston. Alex Hamilton weakly heads out a Johnny Hamilton cross and Wallace smashes home. Dundee leave the field to a chorus of boos at full-time										
30	A	KILMARNOCK		13	L	0-1	0-1		Slater	Hamilton	Stuart	Seith	Ure	Ryden	Penman	Cousin	Waddell	Houston	Robertson
	11/5		*6,000*	2	26			*McInally 16*	*Forysth*	*Richmond*	*Watson*	*Murray*	*McGrory*	*Beattie*	*Black*	*McInally*	*Yard*	*Hamilton*	*McIlroy*
								Ref: J Paterson (Bothwell)	Dundee have won once at Rugby Park since 1934 and only have one shot on target the whole game. Murray slings a cross in from the right which Ure jumps for but misses, so McInally fires past Slater. Slater pushes a McIlroy snapshot onto the bar and saves at the feet of Beattie.										
31	H	THIRD LANARK		11	W	5-2	0-0	Smith 63, 87, Cameron 68, 85, Ryden 79	Slater	Hamilton	Stuart	Ryden	Ure	Brown	Smith	Penman	Cameron	Cousin	**Mackle**
	13/5		**6,000**	*14*	28			*Stenhouse 48, Curran 77*	*Robertson*	*McGillvray*	*davis*	*Spence*	*Little*	*Baird*	*Bryce*	*Goodfellow*	*Stenhouse*	*McMorran*	*Curran*
								Ref: W Mullan (Cardenden)	The wind takes the ball away from Ure and Curran nets for Bill Hiddelston's side. Ryden limps off for 14 minutes but hits the roof of the net on his return. A Smith shot hits the stanchion inside the goal and rebounds out but the referee doesn't signal a goal. Cameron heads in twice.										
32	H	DUNFERMLINE		10	W	1-0	1-0	Cousin 25	Slater	Hamilton	Stuart	Seith	Ure	Brown	Smith	Penman	Cameron	Cousin	Mackle
	16/5		12,000	*8*	30				*Herriot*	*Callaghan*	*Cunningham*	*Thomson*	*MacLean*	*Miller*	*McLindon*	*Smith*	*Paton*	*Sinclair*	*Melrose*
								Ref: J Barclay (Kirkcaldy)	Cousin scores his 50th goal for Dundee when he shoots from just inside the box after a through-ball from Brown. Mackle twice put crosses into the Pars box with no Dundee player there. Jock Stein's men hit the post in the dying minutes and Slater pushes a Paton free-kick round the post										
33	A	FALKIRK		9	W	2-0	2-0	Gilzean 29, Smith 41	Slater	Hamilton	Stuart	Seith	Ure	Brown	Smith	Penman	Gilzean	Cousin	Mackle
	18/5		***2,000***	*13*	32				*Whigham*	*Rae*	*Hunter*	*Pierson*	*Lowry*	*McCarry*	*Thomson*	*Fulton*	*Redpath*	*Maxwell*	*Stewart*
								Ref: F Crossley (Wishaw)	A near deserted Brockville sees the ball bounces off Cousin's knee and Gilzean hits the ball into the air by accident. Whigham leaves it, but the ball drops in under the bar with Lowry tangled up in the Bairns net. Smith strikes home from seven yards after good wing play by Mackle.										
34	H	RANGERS		9	D	0-0	0-0		Slater	Hamilton	Stuart	Seith	Ure	Brown	Penman	Cousin	Waddell	Wishart	Houston
	25/5		17,000	*1*	33				*Ritchie*	*Shearer*	*Provan*	*Greig*	*McKinnon*	*Baxter*	*Watson*	*McMillan*	*Millar*	*Brand*	*Wilson*
	Home		Away					Ref: D Spiers (Uphall Station)	Dundee finish the season playing host to the team who have captured their championship as the Ibrox side have already secured the league flag. Slater has to saves long-range efforts from Baxter and McMillan. Dundee finish a disappointing ninth, 24 point behind Scott Symon's team.										
Average	11,941		13,588																

League Cup – Section 2					F-A	H-T	Scorers, Times, and Referees	1	2	3	4	5	6	7	8	9	10	11
2	A	DUNDEE UTD		L	2-3	2-2	Gilzean 6, 40	Slater	Hamilton	Cox	Brown	Ure	Wishart	Smith	Penman	Cousin	Gilzean	Robertson
	11/8		*25,300*	0			*Carlyle 24, 44, Irvine 84*	*MacKay*	*Gordon*	*Briggs*	*Neilson*	*Smith*	*Fraser*	*Carlyle*	*Brodie*	*Irvine*	*Gillespie*	*Mochan*
							Ref: A Crossman (Edinburgh)	Dundee line up at a revamped Tannadice with new round-neck strips. Gilzean scores Dundee's first goal of the season when he heads home a Robertson cross and is unmarked in the box when he fires home his second. Debutant Slater is unable to stop a late 18-yard strike from Irvine.										
2	H	CELTIC		W	1-0	0-0	Smith 60	Slater	Hamilton	Cox	Seith	Ure	Wishart	Smith	Penman	Cousin	Gilzean	Robertson
	15/8		21,000	2				*Haffey*	*McKay*	*Kennedy*	*Crerand*	*McNeil*	*Price*	*Lennox*	*Gallacher*	*Hughes*	*Murdoch*	*Byrne*
							Ref: W Mullan (Cardenden)	The championship flag is unfurled before the match by Lady Provost McManus. Gilzean's shot scrapes the post in the fifth minute. Smith scores when he latches onto a Kennedy goal-line clearance from a Gilzean shot. Hamilton chests the ball off the line in injury-time from Bryne.										
2	H	HEARTS		L	0-2	0-0		Slater	Hamilton	Cox	Seith	Ure	Wishart	Smith	Penman	Cousin	Houston	Robertson
	18/8		20,000	2			*Hamilton 68, Wallace 70*	*Marshall*	*Rowland*	*Holt*	*Ferguson*	*Barry*	*Cumming*	*Rodger*	*Paton*	*Davidson*	*Wallace*	*Hamilton*
							Ref: W Brittle (Glasgow)	Dundee bans boys' gate after pitch invasion in midweek. Robertson clashes with Jam Tart keeper Marshall in 17 minutes and limps for the rest of the game. Penman hits bar before Hearts score two quick goals from sling shots outside the box. Slater touches a Davidson shot onto the bar.										
2	H	DUNDEE UTD		W	2-1	1-0	Smith 31, 79	Slater	Hamilton	Cox	Seith	Ure	Wishart	Smith	Penman	Cameron	Cousin	Houston
	25/8		19,500	4			*Irvine 49*	*MacKay*	*Gordon*	*Briggs*	*Neilson*	*Smith*	*Fraser*	*Riddle*	*Millar*	*Carlyle*	*Irvine*	*Mochan*
							Ref: W Syme (Glasgow)	Dundee fans chant 'We want Penman' during match and the 19-year-old withdraws his transfer request afterwards. Smith scores his first past future Dees boss Don MacKay in Utd goal when he cuts in from the touchline, shapes to pass but fires in with the wind's help from 35 yards										
2	A	CELTIC		L	0-3	0-1		Slater	Hamilton	Cox	Seith	Ure	Wishart	Smith	Penman	Cameron	Cousin	Robertson
	29/8		*28,000*	4			*Gallagher 1, Hughes 83, 90*	*Haffey*	*McKay*	*Kennedy*	*Crerand*	*McNeil*	*Price*	*Lennox*	*Gallagher*	*Hughes*	*Murdoch*	*Byrne*
							Ref: R Roger (Stonehouse)	Cologne spy Karl Frohlich sees Celtic score immediately when a Crerand lob up the middle was headed out by Ure to Gallacher who rifles in 20 yards out. Hughes beats Ure in the box and shoots into far corner and doubles his tally on time when Ure failed to clear a Kennedy cross.										
2	A	HEARTS		L	0-2	0-0		Slater	Hamilton	Cox	Seith	Ure	Stuart	Smith	Penman	Gilzean	Houston	Robertson
	1/9		*15,000*	4			*Hamilton A 71 (og), Hamilton W 78*	*Marshall*	*Polland*	*Holt*	*Cumming*	*Barry*	*Higgins*	*Wallace*	*Paton*	*Davidson*	*Hamilton W*	*Hamilton J*
							Ref: G Bowman (Clydebank)	Dundee players are convinced that a Gilzean shot which hits the underside of the bar, is a foot over the line but no goal is given. Frohlich again watches Dundee and sees Alex Hamilton deflect a Paton cross behind Slater. Hearts win the section after a Willie Hamilton strike seals the win.										

Qual							
Qual	Hearts	6	4	0	2	11	8	8
	Celtic	6	3	1	2	12	5	7
	Dundee United	6	2	1	3	7	11	5
	DUNDEE	6	2	0	4	5	11	4

Scottish Cup					F-A	H-T	Scorers, Times, and Referees	1	2	3	4	5	6	7	8	9	10	11
1 A	INVERNESS CALEY		8	W	5-1	5-1	Penman 6p, 28, Robertson 35,	Slater	Hamilton	Cox	Seith	Ryden	Wishart	Smith	Penman	Cousin	Gilzean	Robertson
12/1		*4,632*	*5:HL*				*Johnstone 16* [Gilzean 36, Cousin 43]	*Smith*	*Glennie*	*Ross*	*Patience*	*Davidson*	*Christie*	*McLennan*	*MacKenzie*	*Johnstone*	*Reid*	*Munro*
							Ref: S Crossley (Wishaw)	Shankly breaks into Telford Park the night before to check the state of the pitch. With Dundee having lost to Fraserburgh four years before, he was taking nothing to chance. The Dundee players wore rubber boots to combat the conditions. Penman scored penalty after Patience handled.										
2 H	MONTROSE		8	W	8-0	3-0	Cousin 7, 65, Gilzean18, 46, Wishart 31,	Slater	Hamilton	Cox	Seith	Ure	Wishart	Smith	Waddell	Cousin	Gilzean	Robertson
5/2		12,062	*2:14*				[Robertson 68, Waddell 73, Smith 79]	*Grieve*	*Newton*	*Ogilvie*	*Gregal*	*Plenderleith*	*Folan*	*Riddle*	*Dunn*	*Gardiner*	*Wallace*	*McDonald*
							Ref: J Barclay (Kirkcaldy)	Conditions are farcical, with players constantly slipping on the icy pitch. Cousin heads home a Robertson corner. Smith's crosses set up goals for Cousin and twice for Gilzean who returns the compliment for the 38-year-old. Wishart and Waddell both score strikes from outside the box.										
3 H	HIBERNIAN		8	W	1-0	1-0	Gilzean 42	Slater	Hamilton	Cox	Seith	Ure	Wishart	Smith	Penman	Cousin	Gilzean	Robertson
18/3		16,000	*17*					*Wilson*	*Davin*	*McCelland*	*Grant*	*Hughes*	*Leishman*	*Scott*	*Stevenson*	*Baker*	*Baxter*	*O'Rourke*
							Ref: T Wharton (Glasgow)	Gilzean is given some rough treatment from the Hibs. Smith plays a short ball to Cousin but Penman takes over and crosses for Gilzean to head strongly past the stationary Wilson. Dundee wait five minutes at half-time for Hibs to reappear as Mo Stevenson gets three stitches in his head.										
QF H	RANGERS		9	D	1-1	1-1	Penman 44p	Slater	Hamilton	Cox	Seith	Ure	Wishart	Smith	Penman	Cousin	Gilzean	Robertson
30/3		36,839	*1*				*Brand 55p*	*Ritchie*	*Shearer*	*Caldow*	*Greig*	*McKinnon*	*Baxter*	*Henderson*	*McLean*	*Millar*	*Brand*	*Wilson*
							Ref: J Barclay (Kirkcaldy)	Gilzean is taken down in the box and Penman scores from the spot despite gamesmanship from Baxter. Brand scores penalty after he is fouled by Cox. Gers players jostle the referee after he awards a goal and then chops it off for offside after consulting the linesman in the last minute.										
QF A	RANGERS		9	L	2-3	1-1	Gilzean 34, 46	Slater	Hamilton	Cox	Seith	Ure	Wishart	Smith	Penman	Cousin	Gilzean	Robertson
R 3/4		*82,000*	*1*				*Hamilton15 (og), Brand 58p, 88*	*Ritchie*	*Shearer*	*Caldow*	*Greig*	*McKinnon*	*Baxter*	*Henderson*	*McLean*	*Millar*	*Brand*	*Wilson*
							Ref: J Barclay (Kirkcaldy)	Brand lobs the ball down the middles but Hamilton heads it past Slater into his own net. Gilzean heads home a Wishart free-kick after Greig handled. Gilzean smashes in from 18 yards. Brand nets penalty after Hamilton obstructs Wilson and scores after Ure misses a Henderson cross.										

European Cup								1	2	3	4	5	6	7	8	9	10	11
P:1 H	COLOGNE			W	8-1	5-0	Hem'9(og), Wis'11, Rob'12,Gilz'26, 64, 67,	Slater	Hamilton	Cox	Seith	Ure	Wishart	Smith	Penman	Cousin	Gilzean	Robertson
5/9	(W Germany)	25,000					*Hamilton 71 (og)* [Smith 45, Penman 49]	*Ewart*	*Regh*	*Sturm*	*Hemmersbach*	*Weilden*	*Benthaus*	*Thielen*	*Schafer*	*Mueller*	*Habig*	*Harnig*
							Ref: K Jorggensen (Denmark)	Ewart collides with Cousin in the second minute, is dazed and replaced in goal at half-time by defender Regh. Hemmersbach diverts a Penman cross into his own net. Smith, Cousin and Hamilton all cross for Gilzean to head a hat-trick. Hamilton mis-hits a Habig cross past Bert Slater.										
P:2 A	COLOGNE			L	0-4	0-3	*[Ure 57 (og)]*	Slater	Hamilton	Cox	Seith	Ure	Wishart	Smith	Penman	Cousin	Gilzean	Robertson
26/9		*40,000*					*Habig 7p, Muller40, Schaefer 45,*	*Schumachar*	*Polt*	*Regh*	*Schnellinger*	*Weilden*	*Benthaus*	*Thielen*	*Habig*	*Mueller*	*Schafer*	*Harnig*
							Ref: A Poulsen (Denmark) (Dundee win 8-5 on aggregate)	Hamilton palms a Schafer header over the bar and Habig nets the kick. Slater carried off in 27 minutes with a head injury saving at the feet of Mueller who next fires past Penman in goal. Slater returns heavily bandaged and sees a Habig penalty hit the bar after Ure had fouled Thielen.										
1:1 A	SPORTING LISBON			L	0-1	0-0		Slater	Hamilton	Cox	Seith	Ure	Wishart	Smith	Penman	Cousin	Gilzean	Houston
24/10	(Portugal)	*50,000*					*Geo 89*	*Carvalho*	*Carlos*	*Hilario*	*Berides*	*Lucio*	*Julio*	*Hugo*	*Osvaldo*	*Mascargnhas*	*Geo*	*Moras*
							Ref: M Faucheau (France)	Kick-off is delayed five minutes for photographs. Gilzean over-runs the ball when clean through in six minutes. Slater punches a high cross to Geo who shoots towards the near post. Although Slater recovers to tip it onto the bar and Wishart clears off the line, the referee signals a goal.										
1:2 H	SPORTING LISBON			W	4-1	2-0	Gilzean 13, 53, 59, Cousin 45	Slater	Hamilton	Cox	Seith	Ure	Wishart	Smith	Penman	Cousin	Gilzean	Robertson
31/10		32,000					*Figuerido 65*	*Carvalho*	*Lino*	*Hilario*	*Carlos*	*Lucio*	*Julio*	*Figuerido*	*Osvaldo*	*Mascarhenhas*	*Geo*	*Morais*
							Ref: E Olsen (Sweden) (Dundee win 4-1 on aggregate)	Smith beats two men and squares to Gilzean who scores with a low drive from 15 yards. Dundee are lucky to get a corner when Robertson shoots over and Cousin heads home Smith's second cross. Gilzean scores from 25 yards and side-foots a Penman cross home for his hat-trick.										

Rd	Ven	Opponent	Att	Res	Score	HT	Scorers	1	2	3	4	5	6	7	8	9	10	11
QF 1	A 6/3	ANDERLECHT (Belgium)	*60,000*	W	4-1	2-1	Gilzean 1,18, Cousin 47, Smith 67	Slater	Hamilton	Cox	Seith	Ure	Wishart	Smith	Penman	Cousin	Gilzean	Robertson
							Lippens 36p	*Fazekas*	*Heylens*	*Cornelius*	*Hanon*	*Verbiest*	*Lippens*	*Janssens*	*Jurion*	*Stockman*	*Van Himst*	*Puis*
							Ref: M Dienst (Switzerland)											

The match is moved to the Belgian national stadium Heysel after Anderlecht knocked out holders Real Madrid in the last round. From kick-off Gilzean beats Fazekas with a low drive. Cox is penalised for handball and despite showing the ref a mark on his chest, Lippens scores the pen.

Rd	Ven	Opponent	Att	Res	Score	HT	Scorers	1	2	3	4	5	6	7	8	9	10	11
QF 2	H 13/3	ANDERLECHT	40,000	W	2-1	0-1	Cousin 78, Smith 82	Slater	Hamilton	Cox	Seith	Ure	Wishart	Smith	Penman	Cousin	Gilzean	Robertson
							Stockman 30	*Trappeniers*	*Heylens*	*Cornelius*	*Hanon*	*Verbiest*	*Lippens*	*Janssens*	*Jurion*	*Stockman*	*Van Himst*	*Puis*
							Ref: M Dienst (Switzerland) (Dundee win 6-2 on aggregate)											

89 Anderlecht fans see their white and mauve-clad players score when Stockman nets a pass from Belgian player of the year Van Himst. The Dees grow stronger on the muddy surface and their pressure pays off as both Cousin and Smith sweep the ball home late on, just inside the box.

Rd	Ven	Opponent	Att	Res	Score	HT	Scorers	1	2	3	4	5	6	7	8	9	10	11
SF 1	A 24/4	AC MILAN (Italy)	*78,000*	L	1-5	1-1	Cousin 22	Slater	Hamilton	Stuart	Seith	Ure	Wishart	Smith	Penman	Cousin	Gilzean	Houston
							Sani 3, Mora 53, 82, Barison 47, 77	*Ghezzi*	*David*	*Trebbi*	*Benitez*	*Maldini*	*Trapattoni*	*Mora*	*Sani*	*Altafini*	*Rivera*	*Barison*
							Ref: V Caballero (Spain)											

Kick-off is delayed 13 minutes due to the large San Siro crowd. Cousin heads an away goal for Dundee after a fine run from Penman. Milan score all five goals from crosses, as they play high balls on top of Hamilton. The referee is subsequently banned, for accepting gifts from Milan.

Rd	Ven	Opponent	Att	Res	Score	HT	Scorers	1	2	3	4	5	6	7	8	9	10	11
SF 2	H 1/5	AC MILAN	38,000	W	1-0	1-0	Gilzean 44	Slater	Hamilton	Stuart	Seith	Ure	Wishart	Smith	Penman	Cousin	Gilzean !	Houston
								Ghezzi	*David*	*Trebbi*	*Benitez*	*Maldini*	*Trapattoni*	*Mora*	*Pivatelli*	*Altafini*	*Rivera*	*Barison*
							Ref: L Van Nufell (Belgium) (Dundee lose 2-5 on aggregate)											

Fists are thrown by both sets of players when Dundee have a penalty claim rejected. Gilzean is fouled by Benitez. From the free-kick Smith crosses perfectly for Gilzean to head into the net. Gilzean is sent off for a foul on Benitez after suffering 174 minutes of brutal Italian tackling.

			Home					Away					
	P	W	D	L	F	A	W	D	L	F	A	Pts
1 Rangers	34	13	4	0	53	15	12	3	2	41	13	57
2 Kilmarnock	34	12	4	1	55	16	8	4	5	37	24	48
3 Partick Th	34	11	1	5	39	26	9	5	3	27	18	46
4 Celtic	34	10	3	4	33	16	9	3	5	43	28	44
5 Hearts	34	10	4	3	45	26	7	5	5	40	33	43
6 Aberdeen	34	10	2	5	38	19	7	5	5	32	28	41
7 Dundee Utd	34	10	6	1	41	20	5	5	7	26	32	41
8 Dunfermline	34	9	5	3	37	20	4	3	10	13	27	34
9 Dundee	34	9	6	2	39	20	3	3	11	21	29	33
10 Motherwell	34	6	7	4	32	23	4	4	9	28	40	31
11 Airdrie	34	10	0	7	36	33	4	2	11	16	43	30
12 St Mirren	34	6	4	7	32	36	4	4	9	20	36	28
13 Falkirk	34	8	1	8	35	35	4	2	11	19	34	27
14 Third Lanark	34	6	4	7	28	29	3	4	10	28	39	26
15 Queen South	34	6	3	8	20	30	4	3	10	16	45	26
16 Hibernian	34	4	5	8	17	30	4	4	9	30	37	25
17 Clyde	34	6	1	10	25	38	3	4	10	24	45	23
18 Raith Rovers	34	0	4	13	16	48	2	1	14	19	70	9
	612	146	64	96	621	480	96	64	146	480	621	612

Odds & ends

Double wins: (2) Falkirk, St Mirren.
Double losses: (0).

Won from behind: (3) Raith Rovers (a), Anderlecht (h), Third Lanark (h).
Lost from in front: (5) Dundee Utd (a) LC, Third Lanark (a), Clyde (a), Rangers (a) SC, Dundee Utd (h).

High spots: Reaching European Cup semi-final.
Beating Cologne 8-1 at Dens in Dundee's first ever European tie.
Winning 4-1 at home against Sporting Lisbon.
Winning home and away against Anderlecht, beating the Belgians 4-1 in the Heysel Stadium.
Reaching double figures in 10-2 win against Queen of the South.

Low spots: Finishing ninth in the league as defending champions.
Losing 1-5 in the San Siro to Milan in European Cup semi-final.
Losing first ever home league match against Dundee United.
Gilzean's 7 goals v Queen of the South in November was one short of Jimmy McGrory's League record for Celtic of 8 goals in a game in 1928.

Hat-Tricks: (2) Gilzean 2.
Ever Presents : (1) Penman.
Leading Scorer: Gilzean (24).

	Appearances				Goals				
	Lge	LC	SC	Eur	Lge	LC	SC	Eur	Tot
Brown, Craig	4	1							5
Cameron, Kenny	3	2			3				3
Cousin, Alan	30	5	5	8	6		3	4	13
Cox, Bobby	27	6	5	6					
Gilzean, Alan	27	3	5	8	24	2	6	9	41
Hamilton, Alex	30	6	5	8					
Houston, Doug	17	3		3	4				4
Liney, Pat	2								
Mackle, Tommy	3								
McGeachie, George	1								
Penman, Andy	34	6	4	8	10		3	1	14
Reid, Hugh	4								
Robertson, Hugh	16	5	5	5			2	1	4
Ryden, George	9		1		2				2
Seith, Bobby	28	5	5	8					
Slater, Bert	32	6	5	8					
Smith, Gordon	29	6	5	8	3	3	1	3	10
Stuart, Alex	8	1		2					
Ure, Ian	32	6	4	8					
Waddell, Bobby	9		1		4		1		5
Wishart, Bobby	29	5	5	3	1		1	1	3
(own-goals)					3			1	4
21 players used	**374**	**66**	**55**	**88**	**60**	**5**	**17**	**20**	**102**

Bob Shankly's Scottish Championship medal 1961-62

LIST OF SUBSCRIBERS AND VOTES FOR THE MOST IMPORTANT DUNDEE PLAYER 1961-62

Subscriber	Vote	Subscriber	Vote
Bob Anderson	Alan Cousin	Alan Leslie	Alex Hamilton
Colin W Anderson	Bobby Cox	Alan M MacDonald	Alan Gilzean
Grant Anderson	Bobby Cox	Simon Mackenzie	Andy Penman
Brian D Barr	Alan Gilzean	Alan Martin	Alan Gilzean
Colin Barron	Gordon Smith	R Miller-Kelly	Alan Cousin
Colin Blake	Alan Gilzean	Angus MacNeil Milne	Alan Gilzean
Ally Boyle	Alex Hamilton	Jim Milne	Bobby Cox
Dorothy M Brown	Gordon Smith	Mrs C Moffat	
Brian Burt	Alan Gilzean	Alan D Morris	Alan Gilzean
Jim Butler	Alan Gilzean	Billy Morris	Alan Gilzean
Mark Campbell	Bobby Cox	David Morris	Alan Gilzean
Bill Cassidy	Alan Gilzean	Kenneth Oram	Alan Gilzean
Hugh Cassidy	Bobby Cox	Yvonne Osler	Alan Cousin
Derek R Cook	Alan Gilzean	Norrie Price	Alan Gilzean
Andrew Curren	Alan Gilzean	Barry Robertson	Gordon Smith
Grant Dickson	Gordon Smith	Colin Robertson	Gordon Smith
Brian Dunbar	Gordon Smith	George Robertson	Alan Gilzean
John Edwards	Alan Gilzean	Alan Speed	Alan Gilzean
James Geekie	Alan Cousin	Mark Thompson	Alan Gilzean
Donald Gellatly	Alan Gilzean	Steve Watson	Alan Gilzean
Scott Glenday	Bobby Cox	David Weir	Ian Ure
Grahame Guild	Gordon Smith	1ST	ALAN GILZEAN
Chic Haggart	Ian Ure	2ND	GORDON SMITH
Peter Hutchison	Alan Gilzean	3RD	BOBBY COX